About the Author

LUKE PEMBERTON is an independent author of *How to Find Your Way Out When In Despair: a Guide to Rediscovering Your Self-Worth,* and *How To Sort Your Head Out: Build Your Self-Esteem by Understanding Your Emotional Fears,* in which he maps out his own experience of recovering from emotional despair through a series of over 400 drawings. This is his third book. Prior to attempting the perils of writing for a living, he worked in the political department of an international diplomatic organisation dealing with armed conflicts and other international issues.

How To See Religion Differently

Luke Pemberton

SilverWood

Published in 2018 by SilverWood Books

SilverWood Books Ltd
14 Small Street, Bristol, BS1 1DE, United Kingdom
www.silverwoodbooks.co.uk

Copyright © Luke Pemberton 2018

The right of Luke Pemberton to be identified as the author of this work
has been asserted in accordance with the Copyright, Designs
and Patents Act 1988 Sections 77 and 78.

All rights reserved. No part of this publication may be reproduced,
stored in a retrieval system, or transmitted in any form or by any means,
electronic, mechanical, photocopying, recording or otherwise,
without prior permission of the copyright holder.

ISBN 978-1-78132-793-7 (paperback)
ISBN 978-1-78132-794-4 (ebook)

British Library Cataloguing in Publication Data
A CIP catalogue record for this book is available from
the British Library

Page design and typesetting by SilverWood Books
Printed on responsibly sourced paper

For anyone struggling with religious doubt

Contents

	Introduction	9
Part 1	**Sin, shame and submission**	11
	1. This is me	11
	2. Born sick, commanded to be well	13
	3. Religion kept me feeling like a child	32
	4. Breaking point	38
Part 2	**What questioning my religion revealed to me**	44
	1. Scared of doubting my teddy bear of religion	44
	2. Working out exactly what I believed	47
	3. Catholicism also involves some objectionable beliefs	56
	4. Some uncomfortable personal realisations	61
	5. Which bit of being gay is a sin?	69
	6. What makes Jesus' teachings automatically moral?	70
	7. God couldn't organise a booze-up in a brewery	74
	8. And his promotional tactics would be banned these days…	77
	9. God deserves to be 'unfriended'	80
	10. God is like any other emotionally disengaged father	82
	11. Where did all this belief stuff come from anyway?	85
	12. A flimsy edifice?	94
	13. Biblical Christianity is not Catholicism	107
	14. Religion in context – a possibly infinite universe	109
	15. Why do we need God?	118
	16. Many religious messages seem to me harmful for society	120
	17. Religion in charts	123

	18. Religion gets in the way	127
	19. Much better to be an amazing primate than a fallen angel	133
Part 3	**Finding my own way in life**	134
	1. Leaving religion is liberating, but daunting	134
	2. Replacing the false friend of religion	136
	3. Some concluding remarks	138
Part 4	**Selected reading**	139

Introduction

I have suffered from insecurity and very low self-esteem for much of my life. Thankfully, I managed to overcome these fears as detailed in my first two books (*How to Find Your Way Out When In Despair: A Guide to Rediscovering Your Self-worth* and *How To Sort Your Head Out: Build Your Self-Esteem by Understanding Your Emotional Fears*). My period of recovery involved a fair amount of despair and frustration. Luckily, I managed to channel this negative energy into something positive, and I found the courage to question my religious beliefs. (I say courage because I found it at first a frightening thing to do, as I discuss later in this book.) I found this religious doubt initially bewildering. My religious beliefs had seemed to me as certain as day follows night, so why on earth would I question them? I am very glad that I did, because I came to realise, after much reading, discussion and reflection, that my religion, Christianity, was simply implausible to me. This book outlines the process of questioning my religion, what this process revealed to me, and why it was good for my mental health.

I hope readers will forgive a sense of frustration that may come across in these pages. To be frank, realising I had dedicated a large part of my life to a belief system that I now regard as largely irrelevant was an exasperating experience and it was difficult to mask this when writing the book.

Please note, when not specified, all the references in this book to God or religion are references to Catholic Christianity, as I was raised in this system of belief and it is the most familiar to me. However, many of the notions raised in the book could also be applied to the other two Abrahamic religions, namely Judaism and Islam, as well as perhaps other religions.

I very much hope that this book contributes in whatever small way to furthering the debate about a topic that is never far from the news.

Part 1

Sin, shame and submission – realising religion has its downsides

1. This is me

THIS IS ME NOW, MIDDLE-AGED, BUT MY BEER BELLY IS SHRINKING :)

I went to a Catholic convent school from the ages of four to eight, a Church of England school from eight until twelve and then from the ages of thirteen to eighteen I studied theology at A-level at a Catholic boarding school in the

English countryside run by Benedictine monks. As a young boy, the thought of becoming a priest crossed my mind on a few occasions. I continued going to church irregularly until middle age, and often prayed.

A NUN AND ME AT MY JUNIOR SCHOOL

ME BEING GREETED BY A MONK ON THE FIRST DAY AT BOARDING SCHOOL

(ME, KNEELING IN CHURCH)

I WENT TO CHURCH FAIRLY OFTEN IN ADULT LIFE

Otherwise, my life was ordinary. I loved *Star Wars*, football, most other sports, and comics as a kid. I played with my siblings, went through all the usual musical genres that many of us go through, and had summer holidays on windy British beaches with the occasional venture onto the continent, or to our wider family in Ireland. I was single for a very long time and was fortunate to meet a wonderful woman who became my wife, and we now have two lovely children.

2. Born sick, commanded to be well – how religious shame crippled me

One thing that dominated my early life was a deep sense of personal shame. Only in the last few decades has shame been better understood and is now often referred to as the 'master emotion'. Shame is different from guilt in a very profound way, and feeling too much of it, especially in childhood, can overwhelm one's sense of self and cripple one's self-esteem, often for life.

GUILT versus SHAME

I DID SOMETHING BAD

I AM BAD

The late expert on shame, and author of numerous excellent books on the subject, John Bradshaw, talked about shame becoming toxic. This is when

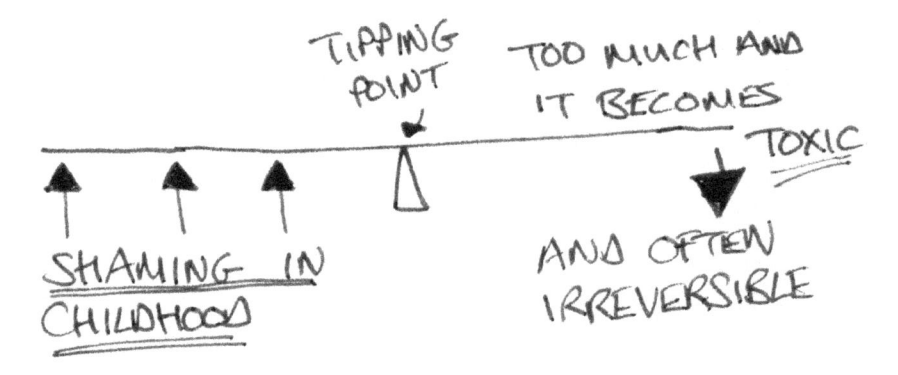

TIPPING POINT

TOO MUCH AND IT BECOMES TOXIC

SHAMING IN CHILDHOOD

AND OFTEN IRREVERSIBLE

a child experiences too much shame, which ends up overwhelming them and "poisoning their soul" (a term coined by the psychologist and child abuse expert, Dr Alice Miller).

I experienced these toxic levels of shame in my childhood, although I wasn't aware of this until I entered therapy in middle age.

The following extract about the effects of excessive shaming on children is taken from my first book, *How to Find Your Way Out When in Despair*.

> Toxic shame eats away at you from the inside out until you are completely hollowed out of any positive emotion. It feels like a cancer of the soul. It then completely fills you up with a feeling of total self-contempt, up to your eyeballs, so that you feel swamped with its effects from the inside out. You become shamed to the core of your being and it overpowers all other emotions you have. It appears at the forefront of your mind every waking moment and poisons every emotional reaction you have with the world. The more it overwhelms you, the greater the self-contempt becomes and the less willing you are to ever help yourself. It then thrives in the world of silence that you create around it. It totally shrinks you as a person in a vicious circle of self-recrimination until you are an emotional black hole. This black hole within you looks to suck in any negative messages it can come across. You become masochistic and look for ways to hurt yourself emotionally. This toxic shame 'parasite' takes you over and feeds on this self-contempt. I therefore often felt that these fears and emotions would engulf me.

Children are often exposed to excessive shaming by their parents (this was certainly the case with me). Toxic shame can lead to a form of confirmation bias: a strong tendency to look for evidence that confirms one's beliefs (in this case, a belief that I was bad to the core). In my experience, Catholicism worsened my sense of shame.

Christianity and shame

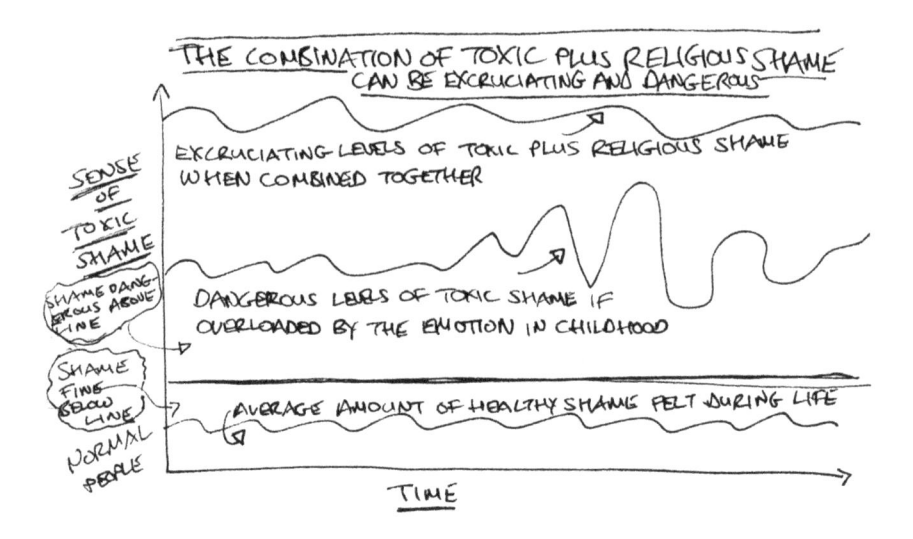

Figure (hand-drawn graph):
- Title: THE COMBINATION OF TOXIC PLUS RELIGIOUS SHAME CAN BE EXCRUCIATING AND DANGEROUS
- Y-axis: SENSE OF TOXIC SHAME
- X-axis: TIME
- Upper curve: EXCRUCIATING LEVELS OF TOXIC PLUS RELIGIOUS SHAME WHEN COMBINED TOGETHER
- Middle line: DANGEROUS LEVELS OF TOXIC SHAME IF OVERLOADED BY THE EMOTION IN CHILDHOOD (SHAME DANGEROUS ABOVE LINE)
- Lower line: AVERAGE AMOUNT OF HEALTHY SHAME FELT DURING LIFE (SHAME FINE BELOW LINE / NORMAL PEOPLE)

Being told as a young child that I was not good enough as I was to receive God's love really affected me.

Figure (hand-drawn cartoon): NUN IN MY FIRST SCHOOL — "LUKE, YOU WERE BORN IN SIN BUT GOD COMMANDS THAT YOU ARE PURE AND GOOD" — "ok..."

As the late Christopher Hitchens so memorably put it, I felt at a young age that I "was born sick but commanded to be well". The fact that I had experienced regular shaming by my parents made me a lot more vulnerable to accusations of shame by the nuns in my convent primary school. At home, I felt that I had disappointed my father and that I was to blame for his disinterest in me. Being told regularly, in school and in church, that God in the form of a man had been tortured and killed because of my sinfulness, further crippled my self-esteem.

> REMEMBER, IT'S YOUR FAULT THAT I HAVE TO BE TORTURED AND EXECUTED!
>
> I FEEL COMPLETE RESPONSIBILITY AND DEEP SHAME FOR WHAT I HAVE EVIDENTLY DONE

> NOW YOU HAVE TO BELIEVE EVERYTHING I SAY ABOUT THIS FAR AWAY LAND WHICH HAD A PRIMITIVE CULTURE AND STRANGE LANGUAGE IN WHICH A MAGIC MAN LIVED WHO COULDN'T BE KILLED. IF YOU DARE TO QUESTION ANYTHING YOU WILL BE PUNISHED. OK, LOVELY BOY?
>
> WOW, SOUNDS LIKE OBI WAN KINOBI FROM STAR WARS (AND I NEED TO BE A GOOD BOY)

A MAN AT MY JUNIOR SCHOOL   A TOTALLY CREDULOUS ME AT 5 YEARS OLD

> OK, JUST BELIEVE IN JESUS, AND OBEY EVERYTHING THE CHURCH SAYS, THEN YOU MIGHT BE ABLE TO JOIN YOUR FRIENDS AND FAMILY IN HEAVEN.
>
> OK, I'LL DO ANYTHING YOU WANT, ALWAYS!

The effects of religious shame

My susceptibility to believing the worst about myself, and my experience of religion, had numerous implications for me.

Submissiveness and shame went together for me.

Because I was so desperate for acceptance, approval and affirmation from my parents and from God, I bought into the very submissive and arguably humiliating language and symbolism of the Catholic Church.

1. NEVER QUESTION OUR AUTHORITY
2. BELIEVE EVERYTHING THE CHURCH SAYS
3. WE HAVE THE FINAL SAY IF YOU ARE WORTHY OF REDEMPTION
4. BEG FOR FORGIVENESS EVERY SUNDAY, IN A PUBLIC DISPLAY OF SUBMISSIVENESS AND SELF CRITICISM
5. DUTY, PIETY, SUBMISSIVENESS, REVERENCE, OBEDIENCE, SACRIFICE, FAITH AND DEVOTION ARE WHAT MAKES A PERSON GOOD AND PURE

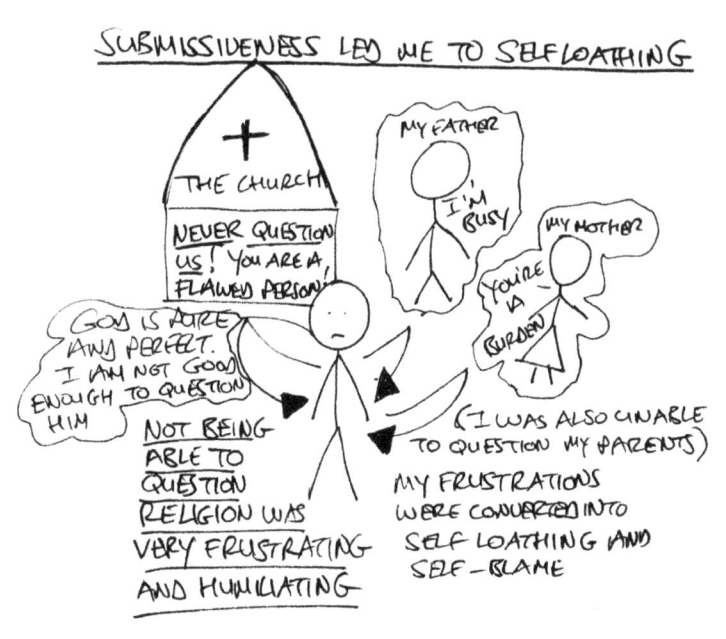

SUBMISSIVENESS LED ME TO SELF LOATHING

THE CHURCH: NEVER QUESTION US! YOU ARE A FLAWED PERSON!

MY FATHER: I'M BUSY

MY MOTHER: YOU'RE A BURDEN

GOD IS PURE AND PERFECT. I AM NOT GOOD ENOUGH TO QUESTION HIM

NOT BEING ABLE TO QUESTION RELIGION WAS VERY FRUSTRATING AND HUMILIATING

(I WAS ALSO UNABLE TO QUESTION MY PARENTS)

MY FRUSTRATIONS WERE CONVERTED INTO SELF LOATHING AND SELF-BLAME

Because of these experiences, I prayed regularly as a child before going to bed, begging God for his forgiveness and for his protection from evil. This later developed into a form of Obsessive Compulsive Disorder (OCD), known as Scrupulosity OCD. I would repeatedly say prayers in my head or murmur them quietly under my breath, especially when I was excited about something (so that it would happen) or scared about something happening (for protection).

An obscene sense of intrusion.

I absolutely believed that God could listen to every thought I had and was always scrutinising my actions to see if I was doing anything wrong. This led to a desperate desire to be perfect and to never think any thoughts I considered would upset him. This is obscenely intrusive, and is mental torture; feeling like you can never be alone with your own thoughts that are permanently being judged.

A real sense of victimisation.

ALL POWERFUL – PERFECT – ALL KNOWING

GOD

NO MATTER HOW HARD YOU TRY TO MAKE AMENDS FOR YOUR TRESPASSES, IT WILL NEVER BE ENOUGH AND I WILL ALWAYS BE ON HAND

(drawing of globe labelled "000,000 Me", "other people on the other side", "poor poor poor")

YOU, LUKE PEMBERTON, I'M WATCHING AND SCRUTINISING YOU ONLY! YOU CANNOT BE TRUSTED. YOU NEED CONSTANT OVERSIGHT BECAUSE YOU ARE A POOR, LOWLY SINNER WHO HAS FAILED HIS PARENTS IN THE MOST FUNDAMENTAL WAY POSSIBLE.

TO PUNISH YOU AT THE SLIGHTEST MISDEMEANOUR. I WILL LET EVERYONE ELSE BE WEAK, SINFUL, AND TREACHEROUS, BUT NOT YOU, WHO WILL NEVER HAVE A MOMENT'S REST FROM MY PERMANENT AND JUDGEMENTAL GAZE. THERE WILL BE NO RESPITE FROM ME AND NO EXPLANATION EVER.

I FELT VICTIMISED, AND WHOLLY UNJUSTIFIABLY SINGLED OUT FOR UNJUST SCRUTINY WHEN I WAS TRYING SO HARD EVERY DAY TO BE AN IDEAL SON AND 'CHILD OF GOD', AND VERY FEARFUL

All resulting in lots of fear.

I became very scared.

Handwritten drawing of a stick figure with a thought bubble containing "GOD" and two small figures, with text around it:

I'M A DISAPPOINTMENT TO MY PARENTS, BUT MOST OF ALL, I'M A WORTHLESS SINNER IN GOD'S PURE AND ALL KNOWING MIND

WORST OF ALL, I'M NOT WORTHY OF REDEEMING MYSELF... ONLY JESUS CAN DO THIS. I FEEL TRAPPED, WORTHLESS, AND HELPLESS

As a result, I looked to God even more to save me, and for him not to forget me or abandon me. I became even more susceptible to Catholic teaching. I was very scared deep down for many years about not being able to join everyone I loved in Heaven after I died, and I was desperate not to give God any reason to bar my entry.

Talk of supernatural experiences was bewildering for me as a child.

I remember well the time a monk, who was also the head teacher, told us during a lesson how he had had an out-of-body experience. He told us how he had felt an urge for his spirit to return to his body as he could feel evil spirits lurking around him trying to infiltrate his body before he reoccupied it. Benedictine monks taught me a variety of subjects, including Theology at A-level (from sixteen to eighteen years of age). As it was a boarding school, we said communal prayers every morning and had to attend high mass every Sunday morning in the school's magnificent cathedral-like abbey.

Confusing religious teachings made matters worse for me.

Contradictions within Catholicism confused me and made me delve deeper into it to try and clarify things.

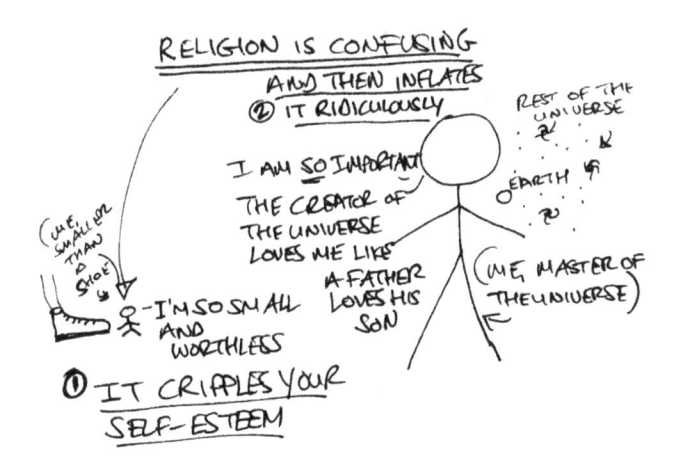

[Hand-drawn illustration: Two house-shaped panels with crosses on top.]

Top panel:
YOU ARE EVERYTHING TO GOD – HE LOVES YOU COMPLETELY
God loves you very much. He gave up his only son so that you could be saved. He has a plan for you and he loves you very much.
(Stick figures labeled "ME AS A CHILD" saying "GREAT!")

Thought bubble: RELIGION WAS A BIT CONFUSING TO ME

Bottom panel:
YOU ARE NOTHING COMPARED TO GOD
But you must be like a slave to him, worshiping him, bowing down to him, recognising you are nothing in your sin compared to his majesty. You must repent and always ask for forgiveness for trespassing against him.
(Stick figures labeled "ME AS A CHILD" saying "UH... OK, I GUESS")

I thanked God for my achievements and blamed myself for any apparent failures.

Whenever I achieved anything in my life I would thank God for granting me the ability to do so. I didn't believe I could succeed without God's help.

Whenever I achieved something in life, I would credit the success to God

> God is so great! I got an A+ in my exam thanks to him! It must be because of all the prayers I said last night.

And whenever I failed at something, I would blame myself severely

> God must be so disappointed in me for failing this exam. I must pray for his forgiveness and try harder.

Toxic shame makes you believe that you are not worthy of help or of being saved from your predicament in any way, so I suffered in silence.

I put a huge amount of pressure on myself as a result and I was very self-critical.

100% PURE / 5 STAR PURITY

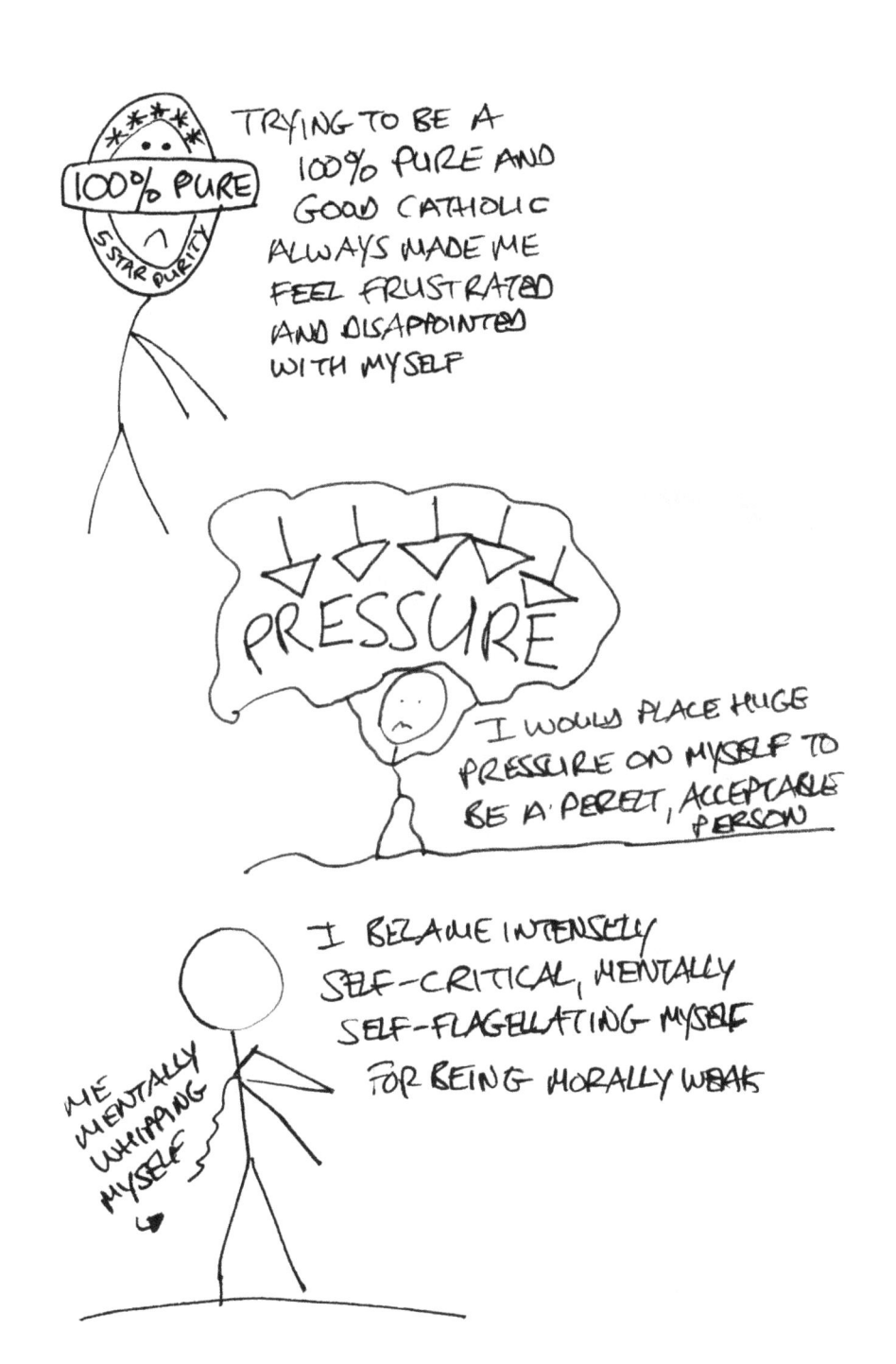

Trying to be a 100% pure and good Catholic always made me feel frustrated and disappointed with myself

PRESSURE

I would place huge pressure on myself to be a perfect, acceptable person

Me mentally whipping myself

I became intensely self-critical, mentally self-flagellating myself for being morally weak

I WOULD INTERPRET RANDOM EVENTS AS SIGNS FROM GOD

I WITNESSED A MINOR TRAFFIC ACCIDENT TODAY. I HAVE OBVIOUSLY BEEN LESS THAN PERFECT RECENTLY AND I MUST DO BETTER...

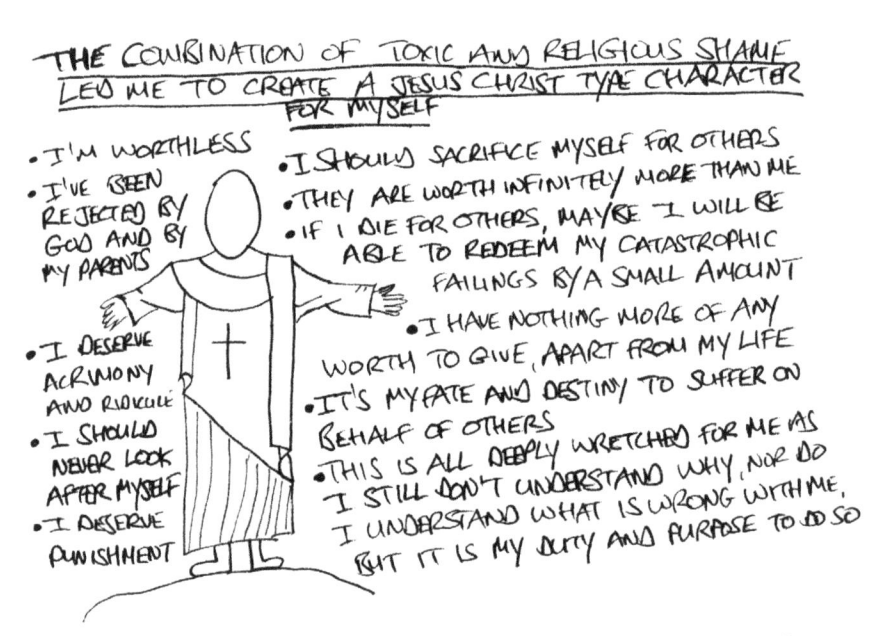

THE COMBINATION OF TOXIC AND RELIGIOUS SHAME LED ME TO CREATE A JESUS CHRIST TYPE CHARACTER FOR MYSELF

- I'M WORTHLESS
- I'VE BEEN REJECTED BY GOD AND BY MY PARENTS
- I DESERVE ACRIMONY AND RIDICULE
- I SHOULD NEVER LOOK AFTER MYSELF
- I DESERVE PUNISHMENT

- I SHOULD SACRIFICE MYSELF FOR OTHERS
- THEY ARE WORTH INFINITELY MORE THAN ME
- IF I DIE FOR OTHERS, MAYBE I WILL BE ABLE TO REDEEM MY CATASTROPHIC FAILINGS BY A SMALL AMOUNT
- I HAVE NOTHING MORE OF ANY WORTH TO GIVE, APART FROM MY LIFE
- IT'S MY FATE AND DESTINY TO SUFFER ON BEHALF OF OTHERS
- THIS IS ALL DEEPLY WRETCHED FOR ME AS I STILL DON'T UNDERSTAND WHY, NOR DO I UNDERSTAND WHAT IS WRONG WITH ME, BUT IT IS MY DUTY AND PURPOSE TO DO SO

THIS WOULD MANIFEST ITSELF IN LOTS OF VERY EMBARASSING AND HUMILIATING WAYS

I OFTEN LOOKED HOW I FELT, STRESSED AND BURDENED

WHICH WAS OF COURSE A BIG TURN OFF FOR WOMEN

—UM, HELLO, AND GOODBYE!

I WOULD RESENT MY NON-RELIGIOUS FRIENDS FOR BEING SO CARE FREE...

HURRAY!

ME

...AND SEEMINGLY UNBURDENED BY LIFE AND ITS APPARENT DEMANDS

My fears and sense of shame extended to that most basic of human desires, sex, while a teenager.

FOR MANY YEARS I BELIEVED (THE VERY NATURAL AND ENJOYABLE) ACT OF MASTURBATION WAS VERY WRONG AND SINFUL

FIGHT THE URGE — I'M GOING CRAZY!

AND IF I DID DO IT, I FELT REALLY BAD ABOUT MYSELF AND PRAYED FOR FORGIVENESS

SO, SO SORRY

THOUGHT CRIME

WOW, SHE IS SO PRETTY... I HATE MYSELF FOR HAVING THESE IMPURE THOUGHTS. I'M A POOR SINNER, AND I HAVE FAILED AGAIN BY THINKING IN A SINFUL MANNER.

> GOD IS SO DISAPPOINTED IN ME
>
> I AM NOW IMPURE AND DIRTY. I'VE ALSO LET DOWN MY PARENTS
>
> WHO WAS THAT LOVELY, PRETTY GIRL YOU MET LAST NIGHT? WE'RE ALL SO JEALOUS

I FELT SO ASHAMED AFTER MY FIRST REAL SEXUAL EXPERIENCE AS A TEENAGER (LOOKING BACK NOW IT WAS A LOVELY EXPERIENCE ON A NICE OCCASION WITH A LOVELY GIRL)

My desire to be a faithful child of God even extended to my irregular moments with young women.

I WOULD EVEN PRAY AT NIGHT EVEN (ON THE RARE OCCASION) I WOULD HAVE COMPANY

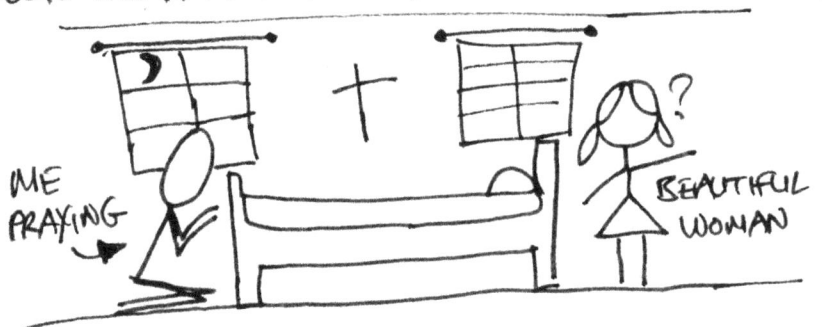

ME PRAYING

BEAUTIFUL WOMAN

I can understand Catholicism's obsession with sex. If religion can obtain a foothold in this fundamental human drive, it gives great leverage to anyone wishing to exploit it.

I would go on to feel like a failure of a man when grown up. I had seemingly so catastrophically let down the two dominant male role models in my life (as well as my mother), just by being me, to the extent that one didn't want to talk to me or see me, and the other had to suffer so much for me. I was also very confused as to what exactly I had done to upset these key figures so much, because I had always tried to please everyone as a child as I was so scared subconsciously of being emotionally abandoned.

Deep down I felt desperate.

All I can do is to be a meek, timid, sorrowful slave to God and hope he finds me worthy of forgiveness, even though I do not deserve it in any way.

3. Religion kept me feeling like a child

Among other things, the language of Catholicism contributed to making me feel like a perpetual child, with the regular use of terms such as 'God the ultimate father', priests and monks in my school as 'fathers', nuns in my junior school as 'sisters', worshippers as 'lambs of God', etc.

The ever-present scrutiny sharpened the feeling that I was a child who couldn't be trusted to get things right without some form of supervision.

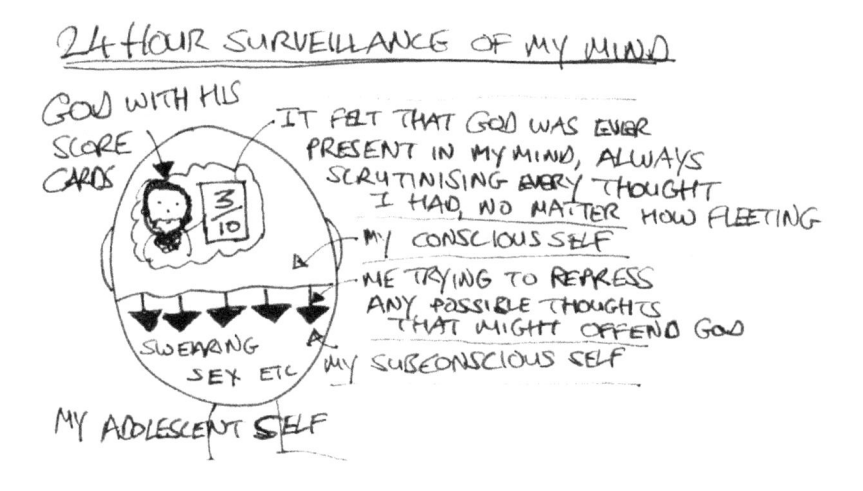

24 HOUR SURVEILLANCE OF MY MIND

- GOD WITH HIS SCORE CARDS
- IT FELT THAT GOD WAS EVER PRESENT IN MY MIND, ALWAYS SCRUTINISING EVERY THOUGHT I HAD, NO MATTER HOW FLEETING
- MY CONSCIOUS SELF
- ME TRYING TO REPRESS ANY POSSIBLE THOUGHTS THAT MIGHT OFFEND GOD
- SWEARING, SEX ETC
- MY SUBCONSCIOUS SELF
- MY ADOLESCENT SELF

Some of the Catholic texts also embedded my view of myself as a child.

THE CATHOLIC BEATITUDES, AND MY BELIEF IN BEING A FALLEN HUMAN, TURNED ME INTO A SMALL MOUSE OF A PERSON (TOGETHER WITH OTHER INFLUENCES)

"I NEED TO BE MEEK, SUFFER IN PATIENCE, PURE OF HEART AND TO BE PERSECUTED FOR THE SAKE OF JUSTICE."

ME, THE MEEK MOUSE

TINY, COMPARED TO THE SIZE OF A NORMAL PERSON'S SHOE

As a result, I was always ready to tell a strange man in a long black dress sitting in an enclosed booth how many times I had masturbated the week before, and to accept his guidance as penance for forgiveness.

ON REFLECTION, KNEELING IN A CONFESSION BOX TELLING A STRANGE MAN IN FUNNY CLOTHES HOW MANY TIMES (WHEN I WAS A YOUNG TEENAGER) I HAD MASTURBATED THE PREVIOUS FEW WEEKS, AND ASKING FOR FORGIVENESS, WAS A BIT WEIRD...

The general approach to worshippers in religion arguably exacerbates the sense of being a child, with the associated feelings of submissiveness.

GOD/JESUS CLEARLY HAS VERY LITTLE CONFIDENCE IN OUR MORALITY

[Illustration: Jesus at a blackboard labeled "10 COMMANDMENTS" and "OTHER RULES", saying "LISTEN CAREFULLY CLASS, YOU CAN'T BE TRUSTED TO FIGURE THIS OUT FOR YOURSELF SO I HAVE TO DO IT FOR YOU, VERY SIMPLY." Labeled "JESUS THE TEACHER", with "GROWN ADULTS AS PUPILS" seated at desks.]

It's an awful way to care for people you claim to love.

WHY DOES GOD HAVE SO LITTLE BELIEF IN US, HIS CREATION?

HE OFTEN REFERS TO US AS SHEEP AND CHILDREN

HE FEELS HE HAS TO SPELL OUT CLEARLY THAT MURDER IS WRONG, IN CASE WE DIDN'T KNOW

"OOPS..."

HE WANTS US TO LIST ALL OUR MISDEMEANOURS REGULARLY TO A PRIEST IN CONFESSION, LIKE CHILDREN DOING HOMEWORK

HE WATCHES OVER US APPARENTLY ALL THE TIME LIKE IN A KINDERGARTEN

God: "I SHOULD HAVE IT CALLED 'KINDER GARTEN' RATHER THAN EARTH"

HE ADOPTS A CARROT AND STICK APPROACH TO ALL OF US

- CARROT: HEAVEN, GOD'S LOVE, GOOD FORTUNE
- HOMO SAPIENS
- STICK: HELL, PUNISHMENT

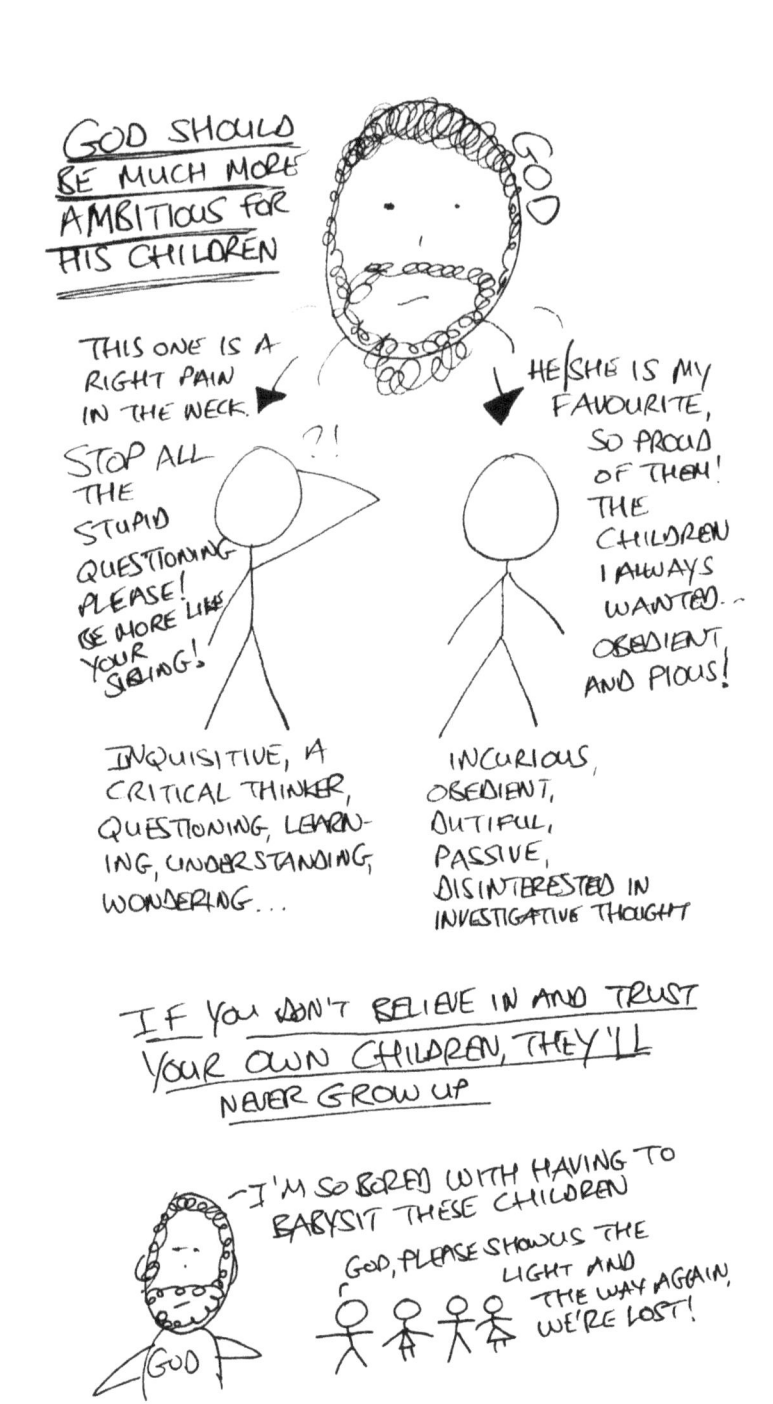

GOD SHOULD BE MUCH MORE AMBITIOUS FOR HIS CHILDREN

GOD

This one is a right pain in the neck. → STOP ALL THE STUPID QUESTIONING PLEASE! BE MORE LIKE YOUR SIBLING!

← **He/she is my favourite, so proud of them! The children I always wanted... obedient and pious!**

Inquisitive, a critical thinker, questioning, learning, understanding, wondering...

Incurious, obedient, dutiful, passive, disinterested in investigative thought

IF YOU DON'T BELIEVE IN AND TRUST YOUR OWN CHILDREN, THEY'LL NEVER GROW UP

GOD: "I'm so bored with having to babysit these children"

"God, please show us the light and the way again, we're lost!"

RELIGION CAN BE VIEWED AS A CHILDISH NOTION

I LOVE REASSURING STORIES!

I DON'T HAVE TO FACE MY FUNDAMENTAL FEAR OF DEATH!

SOMEONE WILL ALWAYS LOOK AFTER ME!

MY DADDY LOVES ME AND HE WILL SAVE ME!

I MUST BEHAVE AS MY DADDY WANTS!

I'LL NEVER BE GOOD ENOUGH FOR HIM AS HE'S AMAZING!

I CAN ~~FEEL~~ GOOD ABOUT MYSELF MERELY BY ASSOCIATION!

MY PERCEPTIONS OF MY FATHER AND GOD MORPHED/MERGED INTO ONE SINGLE PERSONA IN MY MIND

MY FATHER

ALL POWERFUL
CAN DESTROY ME
DISAPPOINTED IN ME
MUCH GREATER THAN ME
RIGHT FOR HIM TO JUDGE ME

HE IS RIGHT TO SACRIFICE ME, FOR THE BENEFIT OF ALL OTHERS, IN A PAINFUL AND HUMILIATING MANNER

I SHOULD NEVER HAVE THE GALL TO QUESTION HIM — HE WORKS IN MYSTERIOUS WAYS

I AM WORTH NOTHING COMPARED TO HIS MIGHT

I BECAME VERY FRIGHTENED OF THIS CHARACTER

Being treated like a child makes one behave like a child, and hang onto childish beliefs and notions.

I HELD ONTO RELIGION LIKE A TEDDY BEAR FROM CHILDHOOD. THIS TEDDY BEAR MADE ME, MOSTLY, FEEL SECURE AND LOVED. IF ANYONE OFFENDED MY TEDDY BEAR LATER IN LIFE, I WOULD TAKE IT VERY PERSONALLY AND GET OFFENDED.

4. Breaking point

My childhood experiences had implications for my adulthood.

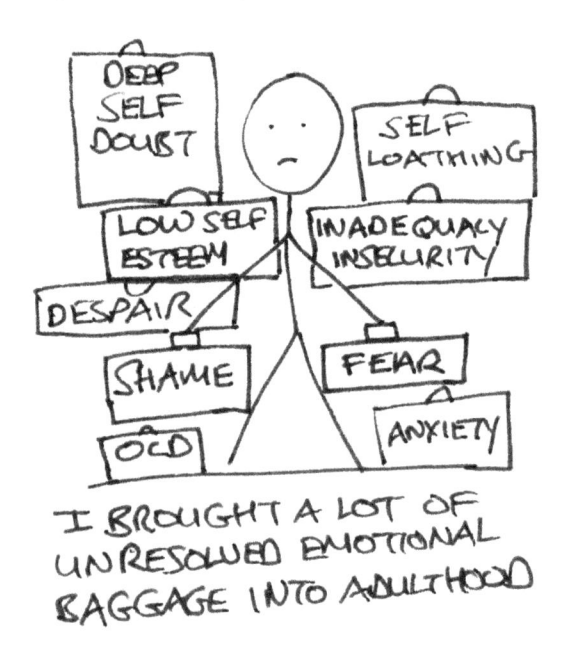

I BROUGHT A LOT OF UNRESOLVED EMOTIONAL BAGGAGE INTO ADULTHOOD

(Deep Self Doubt, Self Loathing, Low Self Esteem, Inadequacy, Insecurity, Despair, Shame, Fear, OCD, Anxiety)

These implications included several burnouts and depressive episodes in middle age.

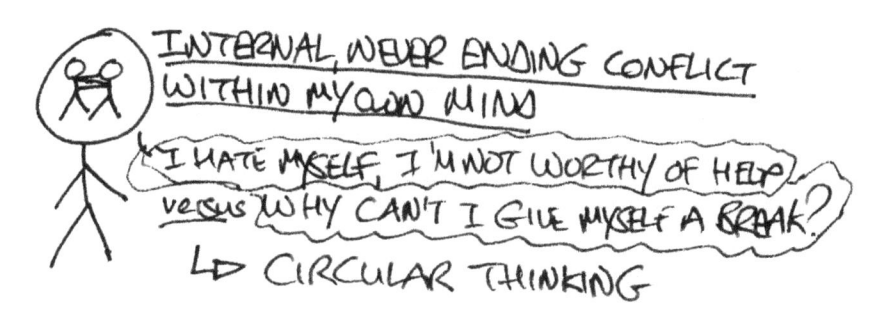

HOW MY BURNOUTS CAME ABOUT

MANIC THINKING SINCE CHILDHOOD

"??!X!" — "IF MY PARENTS DON'T LIKE ME, THEN NOBODY WILL. I'M REALLY SCARED!"

INTERNAL, NEVER ENDING CONFLICT WITHIN MY OWN MIND

"I HATE MYSELF, I'M NOT WORTHY OF HELP" versus "WHY CAN'T I GIVE MYSELF A BREAK?"

↳ CIRCULAR THINKING

A PERPETUAL DESIRE TO BE PERFECT

10/10 100%

"I MUST PROVE MY WORTH CONTINUOUSLY, WITHOUT A PAUSE, OTHERWISE I WILL BE HATED AND ABANDONED, WHICH IS TOO SCARY TO CONTEMPLATE"

NEVER ENDING INTERNAL CONFUSION

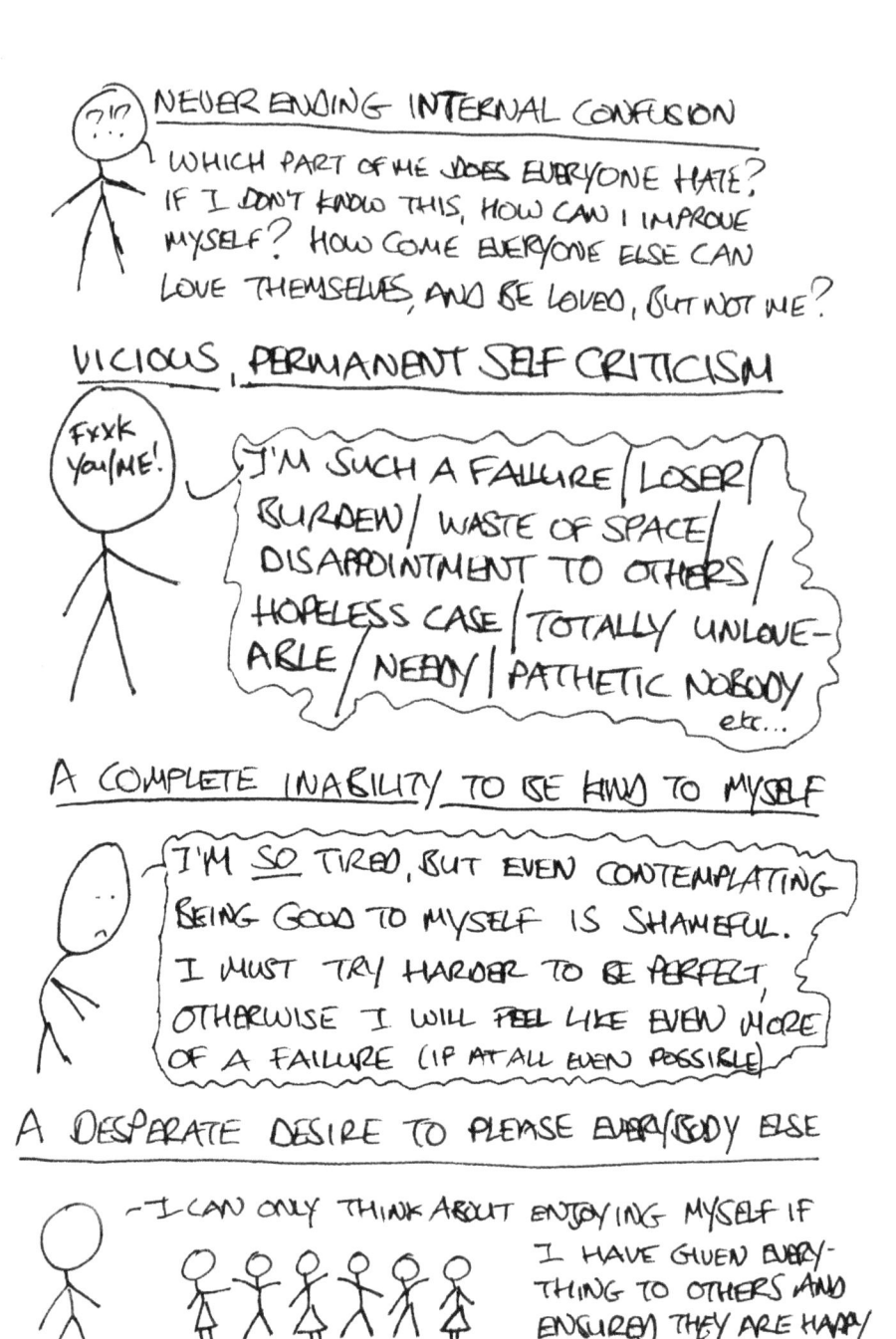

(?!?) WHICH PART OF ME DOES EVERYONE HATE? IF I DON'T KNOW THIS, HOW CAN I IMPROVE MYSELF? HOW COME EVERYONE ELSE CAN LOVE THEMSELVES, AND BE LOVED, BUT NOT ME?

VICIOUS, PERMANENT SELF CRITICISM

(Fxxk you/me!) I'M SUCH A FAILURE / LOSER / BURDEN / WASTE OF SPACE / DISAPPOINTMENT TO OTHERS / HOPELESS CASE / TOTALLY UNLOVEABLE / NEEDY / PATHETIC NOBODY etc...

A COMPLETE INABILITY TO BE KIND TO MYSELF

I'M SO TIRED, BUT EVEN CONTEMPLATING BEING GOOD TO MYSELF IS SHAMEFUL. I MUST TRY HARDER TO BE PERFECT, OTHERWISE I WILL FEEL LIKE EVEN MORE OF A FAILURE (IF AT ALL EVEN POSSIBLE)

A DESPERATE DESIRE TO PLEASE EVERYBODY ELSE

— I CAN ONLY THINK ABOUT ENJOYING MYSELF IF I HAVE GIVEN EVERYTHING TO OTHERS AND ENSURED THEY ARE HAPPY

LONG PERIODS OF INSOMNIA OVER 20 YEARS

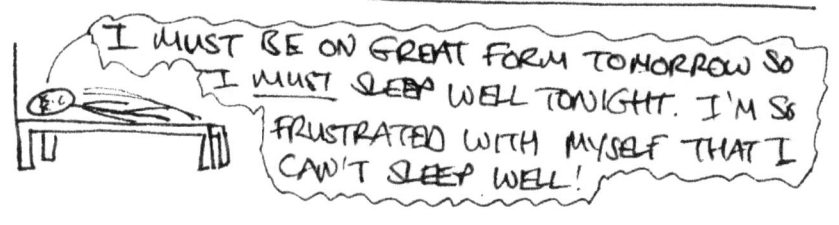

I must be on great form tomorrow so I MUST sleep well tonight. I'm so frustrated with myself that I can't sleep well!

PLUS THE USUAL PRESSURES OF LIFE

WORK, KIDS, WIDER FAMILY, MONEY WORRIES

(AND TOO MUCH BOOZE FOR SELF-MEDICATION)

I need more...

CULMINATING IN A VICIOUS CIRCLE OF THINKING

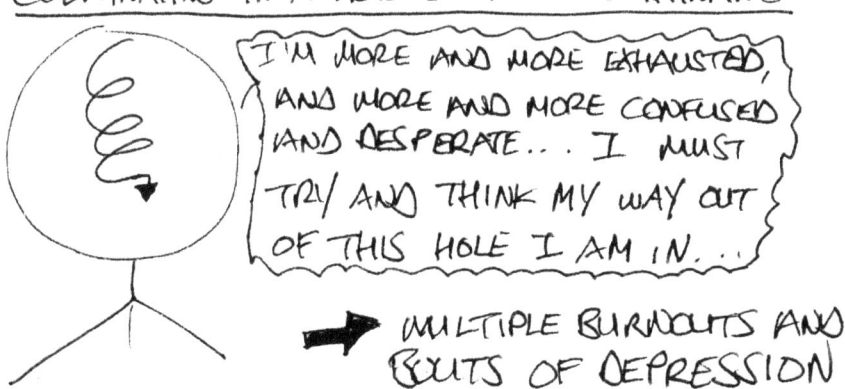

I'm more and more exhausted, and more and more confused and desperate... I must try and think my way out of this hole I am in...

→ MULTIPLE BURNOUTS AND BOUTS OF DEPRESSION

Timber!

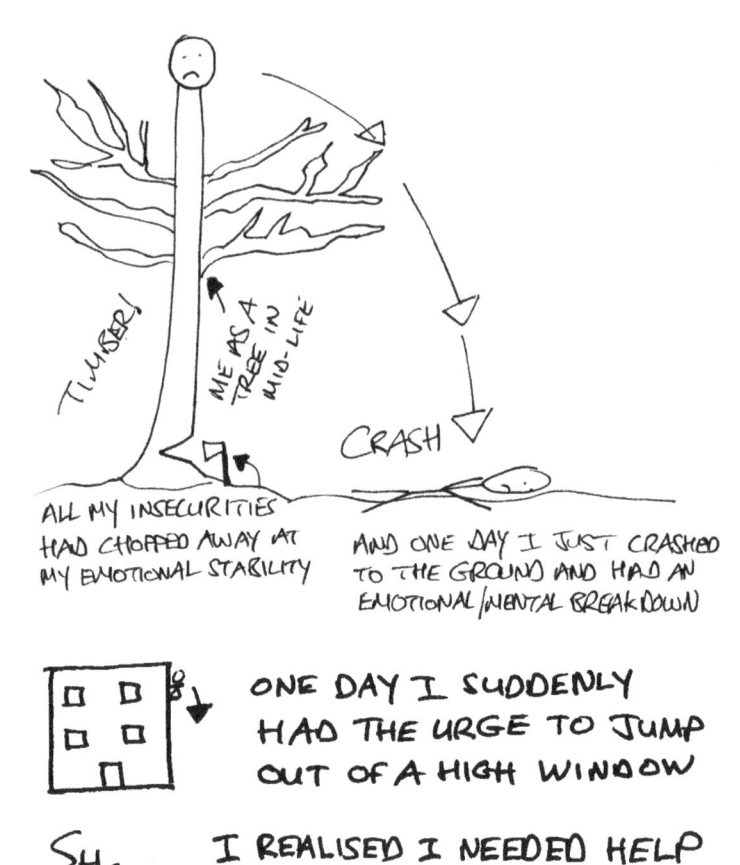

[Drawing of a tree with a sad face, branches being chopped]
TIMBER!
ME AS A TREE IN MID-LIFE
CRASH

ALL MY INSECURITIES HAD CHOPPED AWAY AT MY EMOTIONAL STABILITY

AND ONE DAY I JUST CRASHED TO THE GROUND AND HAD AN EMOTIONAL/MENTAL BREAKDOWN

[Drawing of a building with windows]
ONE DAY I SUDDENLY HAD THE URGE TO JUMP OUT OF A HIGH WINDOW

SHR,"* I REALISED I NEEDED HELP
Why do they call them that?

I went to see a psychotherapist for a few years, which was helpful.

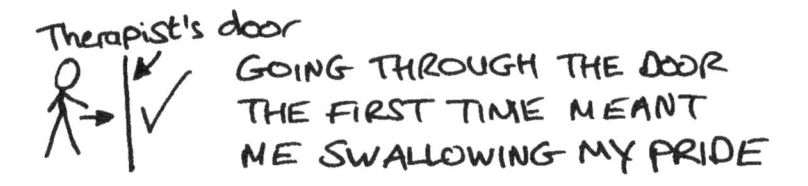

Therapist's door
[Stick figure going through a door]
GOING THROUGH THE DOOR THE FIRST TIME MEANT ME SWALLOWING MY PRIDE

This involved examining the roots of my personality, formed primarily in childhood.

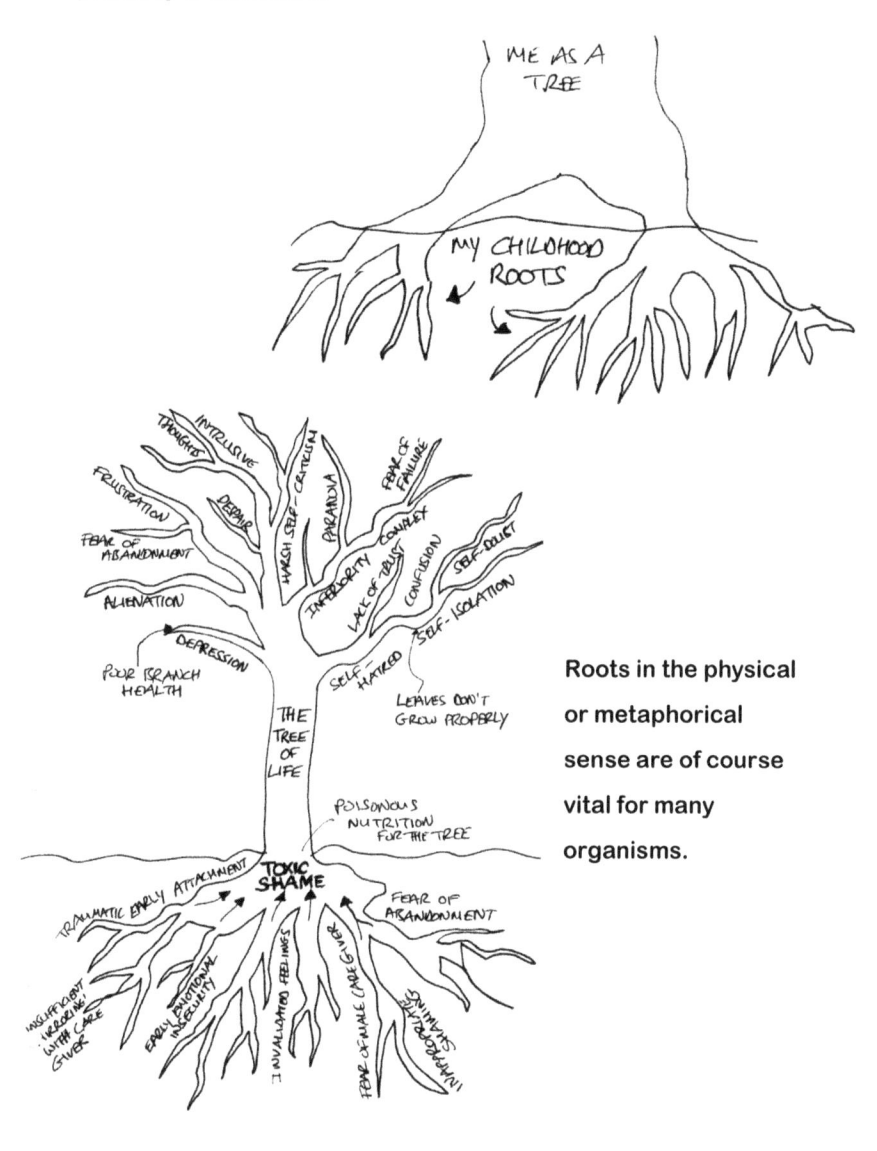

Roots in the physical or metaphorical sense are of course vital for many organisms.

I managed to build up a reasonably good picture of how my personality had developed and I made careful notes of everything I had learned.

Part 2

What questioning my religion revealed to me

1. Scared of doubting my teddy bear of religion

DON'T ATTACK MY TEDDY BEAR!
COMFORTED ME AS A CHILD, COMPANION, SENSE OF SECURITY
MY RELIGIOUS BELIEFS FROM CHILDHOOD

My breakdown eventually forced me to question my religious beliefs, which felt very uncomfortable and illogical – it was like suggesting to myself that my teddy bear of religion was in fact very bad for me. It also felt very morally wrong, sinful, ungrateful, rude and offensive to question the God I believed was my almighty superior, who had given me my life and everything in it. I feared I might lose him as I had lost my parents emotionally as a child.

?! I FEEL REALLY SCARED TO CLICK, BUY NOW

BUY NOW? GOD IS NOT GREAT

WHEN ADDRESSING MY FEARS AND INSECURITIES, I FELT I HAD TO AT LEAST CONSIDER MY RELIGIOUS BELIEFS

This is one of the benefits of energy-sapping psychotherapy. It can bring out lots of latent and buried fear, anger and frustration, which I tried to channel into questioning intensely all the forces that had influenced my life, from my parents to religion. I found this very frightening, especially when it came to take a critical look at my religious beliefs. I had to try very hard to overcome my fear of doing so, a fear of committing a very immoral, disobedient, disrespectful, shameful act, which could lead to serious retribution for me.

GOD — THE FATHER
JESUS — THE SON
THE HOLY GHOST
MARY — MOTHER OF GOD

I FOUND THIS VERY DAUNTING TO SAY THE LEAST

LITTLE ME, THE HUMBLE LAMB →

I HAD TO FIND THE COURAGE TO QUESTION THE VALIDITY AND TRUTH OF CHRISTIANITY AND OF THESE 'SUPREME BEINGS' WHO COULD APPARENTLY SAVE OR DESTROY ME FOR ETERNITY

I managed to pluck up the courage and override these fears.

> HELP! THIS IS SCARY AND FEELS WRONG!
>
> RELIGIOUS DEBATES YouTube

I READ A LOT OF BOOKS ON RELIGION AND WATCHED LOTS OF RELIGIOUS DEBATES, AND FELT VERY SCARED EVEN QUESTIONING MY RELIGIOUS BELIEFS

I recommend these two books, by Christopher Hitchens and Richard Dawkins respectively.

MY BREAKING BAD HANK/TOILET MOMENT

ME ON THE TOILET

WHEN I FIRST REALISED THAT RELIGION HAD IN FACT BEEN A CONTRIBUTORY FACTOR TO MY VERY LOW SELF-ESTEEM AND EMOTIONAL FEAR AND CONFUSION, I FELT LIKE HANK IN BREAKING BAD WHEN HE FINALLY REALISED HIS FRIEND, WALTER WHITE, WAS HIS ENEMY

GOD IS NOT GREAT BY CHRISTOPHER HITCHENS

(*Breaking Bad* was a TV show produced from 2008 to 2013 in which a US high school chemistry teacher, Walter White, diagnosed with inoperable lung cancer, turns to manufacturing and selling methamphetamine in order to secure his family's future. His brother-in-law, Hank, happens to be an officer in the US Drug Enforcement Agency.)

QUESTIONING GOD AFTER YEARS OF BELIEF REQUIRES COURAGE AND TENACITY

HANG GLIDER

FACING HARSH REALITY

NO ONE WILL SAVE ME — ONLY I CAN DO THAT

LOSING LIKE-MINDED COMMUNITY

WALKING INTO HEADWIND OF CONVENTION

ACCEPTING YOU WILL NOT GO TO HEAVEN, AND DEATH IS FINAL

OVERCOMING REAL FEAR OF DIVINE RETRIBUTION

COURAGE TO QUESTION DEEPLY HELD BELIEFS

→ OR STAY OVERWHELMED BY COMFORTING DELUSIONS

FREEDOM
SELF-RESPECT
TRUE INDEPENDENCE OF THOUGHT AND ACTION
NO LONGER A CHILD OR SHEEP
CLARITY OF THOUGHT
REAL LIBERATION
RENEWED LOVE OF THIS, OUR ONLY LIFE
FONDNESS AND RESPECT FOR OTHERS WHO HAVE OVERCOME RELIGIOUS BELIEF

2. Working out exactly what I believed and realising that Catholicism is in fact a bit weird

I tried to take a very objective look at what exactly my belief in Catholicism contained. Without wishing to be too flippant, I realised there were a few rather bizarre concepts within the religion. These included:

[Drawing: a stick figure in priestly robes with a cross, labeled:]

MAGIC MEN!
MAGIC WORDS!
e.g. (SOLEMN BLESSING #9 (ORDINARY TIME) IN THE ROMAN MISSAL)
MAGIC! HANDS THAT CAN BLESS

A belief that men, after studying ancient texts, can somehow endow someone with a beneficial power of protection, just by saying some magic words to them in their presence.

[Drawing: a stick figure wizard with pointed hat holding a wand and a wafer, with two bottles labeled WINE and BLOOD:]

MAGICIANS!
WHO CAN TURN WAFERS INTO HUMAN FLESH... THE BODY OF CHRIST / THE EUCHARIST
AND WINE INTO BLOOD

A belief that these magic men can also turn thin wafers consisting of wheat and water, and wine into the body and blood of someone who died 2,000 years ago, thousands of miles away.

Mount Sinai / The Mount of Olives

MAGIC MOUNTAINS!

A belief that bits of land should be revered, such as Mount Sinai where the Ten Commandments were allegedly given to Moses by God.

MAGIC WATER!

CHRISTENING

ON A BABY'S HEAD EQUALS GOD WILL NOW LOOK AFTER YOU (BUT NO MAGIC WATER AND GOD MAY REGARD YOU AS NOT WORTH HELPING)

A belief that sprinkling holy water (normal water which a priest has spoken to, turning it into holy water) onto a baby's head turns them into a child of God and frees them from the power of darkness inherited because of Adam and Eve eating the forbidden fruit. This practice seems to be the Catholic version of the Jewish naming ceremony and circumcision of newborn boys known as a *bris*. (Newborn Jewish girls are simply bestowed with a Hebrew name.)

REALLY COOL BADDIES!

I believed that the devil was lurking around and could infiltrate me somehow if I wasn't careful and good. Why doesn't God just defeat Satan once and for all? In the Old Testament God is responsible for mass murder and genocide, plus other awful crimes against humanity, likely killing millions. I wonder what the worst thing is that Satan has done in comparison?

TALKING SNAKES!!

I accepted without question the story of the Garden of Eden and that an animal had the ability not only to speak the correct language of the time, but also the psychological and linguistic ability to convince a human being to commit a mortal sin. I also believed it was the woman's fault, as she allegedly shared the fruit with Adam.

INCREDIBLE FRUIT — DELICIOUS, AND FULL OF KNOWLEDGE

It never occurred to me that God was angry that Adam and Eve had, in effect, gained knowledge against his will.

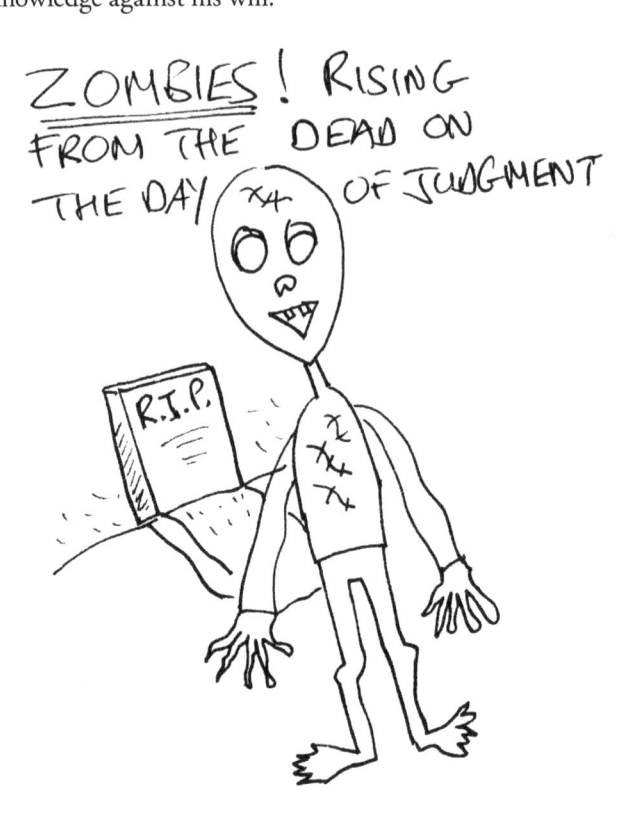

> ZOMBIES! RISING FROM THE DEAD ON THE DAY OF JUDGMENT

I had never considered what the 'resurrection of the dead' would mean in practice. I had stated my belief in this event every week in mass for many years. Jesus also spoke of this event. I can only guess how utterly terrifying it must be for long-dead people to suddenly come back to life again. I assume the clothes they were buried in would have disintegrated into nothing in the ground, adding nakedness to the shock their resurrection would cause. So many other questions spring to mind: would they be hungry and thirsty (I guess so)? What mental state would they be in (pretty freaked out)? What if they didn't want to be alive again (could they commit suicide if they so wished)?

Could they still have children? What would happen to them if they committed mortal sins after resurrection – would they immediately be dead in their grave again? Could they grow new limbs if one had been chopped off before dying? If so, what happened to the previously existing limb? I know these questions sound ridiculous, but if Catholicism preaches such an incredible feat, then the Church must be ready to provide some follow-up answers.

AN AMAZING (STEP-?) BROTHER (JESUS)

IF GOD IS MY FATHER, JESUS IS HIS SON, THEN I GUESS JESUS IS LIKE A BROTHER TO ME?

I didn't realise that the Gospel of Matthew stated that Jesus had brothers (although in what sense I'm not sure).

AN AMAZING (STEP-?) FATHER (GOD)

(NOT SURE IF HE HAD A WIFE? HE HAS A SON, JESUS, SO MAYBE?)

I also never questioned what came before God? If God is so amazing, he must have stemmed from something. Some life forms can reproduce asexually, but I wouldn't classify God in the same way...

AN AMAZING SUPER-HERO (HALF-BROTHER?)
WHO CAN MAKE ANYONE/ANYTHING HOLY
HOLY SPIRIT
I THINK HE'S A BIT LIKE GOD'S MESSANGER, HIS DEPUTY (VICE-GOD, ENFORCER, WHO ZAPS PEOPLE WITH GOD'S LOVE AND ENERGY, BUT WHO IS MOSTLY INVISIBLE, AND IS GUIDED BY GOD, A BIT LIKE REMOTE CONTROL...

Or does he/she/it look and behave just like a ghost?

GHOSTS!
THE HOLY GHOST OR SPIRIT
FLYING BABIES!
ANGEL

I never really questioned the existence of angels either. Are these like fairies and if so where do fairies come from? If not, how come angels exist and fairies don't (it would seem plausible that one form of miniature flying human-like creature could also entail other forms existing)? If they are young, are they underdeveloped mentally? Where do they come from? Do angels reproduce, and if so, are they allowed to have abortions in the case of a deformed foetus angel?

When Jesus and Mary ascended into heaven, did they have to leave the earth's atmosphere? If so, how did they survive the cold of space? What sort of propulsion system did they use to combat gravity? Could this propulsion energy be obtained for human use? If it's 4.5 light years to the nearest star, how far away is heaven?

I believed that I was eating the actual flesh and drinking the blood of Jesus Christ when taking communion in church. Does this make me a cannibal? How much flesh and blood did/does Jesus have if a billion Christians are eating and drinking bits of him every Sunday? Surely, we are just eating replica flesh and drinking replica blood, as he needs his actual body for when he returns to the earth? If so, where does all this excess flesh and blood come from, and if it's not from his body, isn't it fake?

3. I realised that Catholicism also involves some objectionable beliefs

As well as the above rather strange notions, I also came to realise that Catholicism relies on some objectionable claims and notions.

As has been pointed out by numerous commentators, isn't scapegoating immoral? What about the moral requirement for taking individual responsibility for one's actions? If you have no regret for your transgressions, how can just throwing all of these onto someone else, and forcing them away from wherever you are, be in anyway justifiable? And anyway, how can you place or transfer wrongdoing in a practical sense?

COMPULSORY LOVE!
(LOVE WHAT YOU ALSO FEAR)

[Illustration: A robed figure with arms outstretched says: "LOVE ME, PRAISE ME, WORSHIP ME, FOLLOW ME. I'M FULL OF LOVE AND CARE FOR YOU, MY CHILD, AND I WILL LOVE YOU FOREVER, ALWAYS (AND IF YOU DON'T, I'LL SEND YOU TO HELL FOREVER)." A small stick figure replies: "UM, OK… I LOVE YOU! (AND I'M REALLY SCARED OF YOU AT THE SAME TIME)"]

This is just weird.

[Illustration: A tree with apples and a snake. Two stick figures stand beside it. Caption: "ADAM AND EVE ATE FROM THE TREE OF KNOWLEDGE BECAUSE OF A TALKING SNAKE"]

Among these beliefs is the bizarre notion of inherited sin and the belief that all subsequent generations are shamed into obedience because of this obviously mythical event. Apart from the weird story, how is this in any way moral? Surely God knew this was going to happen, so why did he create Adam and Eve in the first place if he knew they were just going to disappoint him? And how can fruit contain knowledge? If Adam and Eve had eaten all the apples, would they have had brains like Einstein? And what is God doing putting knowledge into bits of fruit? Did different apples contain knowledge of random topics or was there some order, like an encyclopaedia? Was this knowledge of yet-to-be discovered topics or just basic knowledge available at the timer? And what's wrong with a bit of knowledge anyway? In addition, the founding stories of some peoples or cultures are regarded by some as rather ridiculous (e.g. The Aboriginal Dreamtime stories). This now seems hypocritical to me.

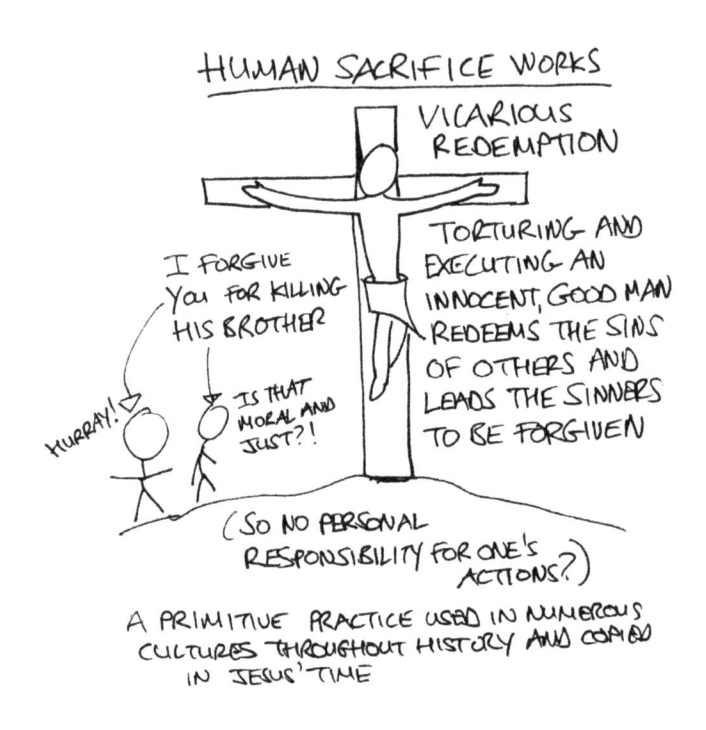

HUMAN SACRIFICE WORKS

VICARIOUS REDEMPTION

TORTURING AND EXECUTING AN INNOCENT, GOOD MAN REDEEMS THE SINS OF OTHERS AND LEADS THE SINNERS TO BE FORGIVEN

I FORGIVE YOU FOR KILLING HIS BROTHER

HURRAY!

IS THAT MORAL AND JUST?!

(SO NO PERSONAL RESPONSIBILITY FOR ONE'S ACTIONS?)

A PRIMITIVE PRACTICE USED IN NUMEROUS CULTURES THROUGHOUT HISTORY AND COPIED IN JESUS' TIME

This is a primitive, disgusting and immoral notion. What's God's thing with human sacrifice? Is he some form of sadist? Why couldn't he just accept a heartfelt apology from humankind (for something they didn't do) rather than demanding the brutal torture and execution in excruciating agony of his own son? And what does he do with other sacrifices anyway; put them on his mantelpiece or on his wall like the stuffed heads of dead animals?

THE APOCALYPTIC NATURE OF THE THREE ABRAHAMIC RELIGIONS WHICH ALL LOOK FORWARD TO THE END OF DAYS, THE SECOND COMING, JUDGMENT DAYS, AND THE EARTH AND EVERYTHING IN IT BEING "LAID BARE"

THE END!

THIS SOUNDS LIKE SOMETHING ONLY THE DEVIL WOULD DO!

FOLLOWED BY THE RAPTURE

TO HEAVEN FOR EVER

WHOOSH!

A DESTROYED AND DESOLATE EARTH, FULL OF UNBELIEVERS?

LIKE THE END OF A JAMES BOND MOVIE WHERE THE HEROES ESCAPE THE MAD MAN'S LAIR

What type of loving God would like to destroy his own, staggeringly complex and beautiful creation, like a spoiled child bored with his toys? And how would he calculate when this would happen? What if he regretted doing it afterwards, would he be able to undo it? What would happen on earth the day after judgment day and the rapture? What if I was eligible for the rapture but I wanted no part of it? Can you opt-out of the rapture? And what about future generations? And why should we be environmentally protective if God is just going to blow the whole place up anyway? Maybe that's why some evangelical Christians don't care about global warming.

> AN INVISIBLE BOSS
> WHO IS EVERYWHERE, AND
> WHO CAN SEE AND HEAR,
> AND DO THINGS ANYWHERE,
> (AND EVERYWHERE)
> ALL AT THE SAME TIME
>
> ?

If God is everywhere, but can't be seen, heard, touched or sensed in any other way, does that mean he has no physical form? How then does he see or hear – wouldn't light and sound waves just pass straight through him? And when people say God is in my heart, what use is this, as the heart has no consciousness? Shouldn't God be in people's brains? And if he is in our brains, what does he do when we are thinking about sex? Does he just turn away for a bit? Why doesn't he stop people committing premeditated murder if he is in their brain when they are about to commit such an act?

If God can see through buildings, I guess we must appear transparent to him? If he can hear everything, how does he differentiate between the thousand prayer murmurings in a big cathedral?

> IT'S SIMPLY FOOLISH TO THINK AN AMAZING, SUPERNATURAL BEING WOULD REVEAL HIMSELF TO A SINGLE MAN VIA:
>
> MOSES — A BURNING BUSH
> JACOB — A DREAM ABOUT A LADDER
> MARY — A FLYING BABY/ANGEL
>
> RATHER THAN SIMPLY TO EVERYONE
>
> (BUT I CAN SEE WHY AN INDIVIDUAL WOULD CLAIM HE/SHE HAS SEEN/HEARD GOD)

> GOD MAKES DISRESPECTFUL AND UNWARRANTED DEMANDS
>
> Amount of Blind Trust Demanded For A Claim — 100%
>
> By a decent, normal, respectful person: I RESPECT YOU ENOUGH NOT TO DEMAND ANYTHING UNREASONABLE FROM YOU
>
> By God: I DEMAND THAT YOU BELIEVE ME, ON PAIN OF DEATH! FOR ALL OF ETERNITY (P.S. I LOVE YOU SO MUCH)

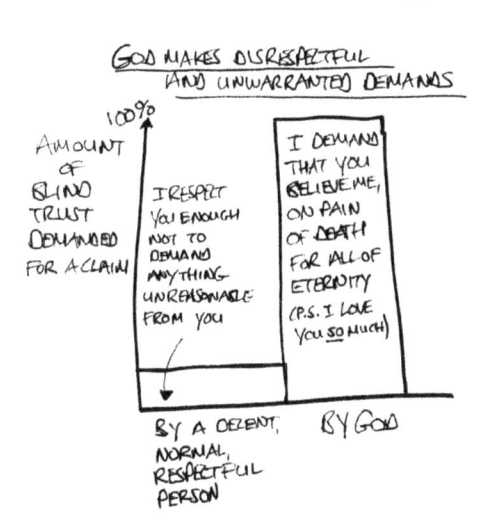

4. Some uncomfortable personal realisations

I also started to come to some inescapable conclusions about the nature and apparent behaviour of the Christian God – conclusions that were often difficult for me as a former believer to arrive at; such was my firm belief in Christianity.

[Cartoon: Heaven scene with Holy Spirit, God, and Jesus on a cloud labelled "HEAVEN". Jesus says: "LOOK DAD/ME, THEY ARE FIGHTING OVER US/ME AGAIN. FANCY WATCHING IT AGAIN? WANT TO BET THIS TIME WHO WINS? THEY ARE SUCH STRANGE CREATURES, HUMANS!"]

WHY DID GOD STAND BY AS THOUSANDS UPON THOUSANDS OF PEOPLE KILLED AND DIED FOR RIVAL INTERPRETATIONS OF WHAT HE SAID?

[Below, labelled EARTH: stick figures shouting "FOR CHRIST!" (PROTESTANTS) vs "FOR CHRIST!" (CATHOLICS); another pair "BURN THE WITCH!"; THE CRUSADES with a shield.]

If God is everywhere, he's clearly doing nothing to stop the carnage he has unleashed when rival interpretations of his own teachings lead to mass bloodshed, such as in the Middle Ages. (After all, people were/are killing each other in a desperate attempt to do his bidding.)

[Cartoon titled "IF GOD MOVED IN NEXT DOOR": A figure at the door says "Hi!, I'M YOUR'E NEW NEIGHBOUR. I LOVE YOU SO MUCH THAT I JUST ARRANGED FOR MY SON TO BE EXECUTED FOR YOU, PRETTY IMPRESSIVE, EH!? YOU CAN DRINK HIS BLOOD AND EAT HIS FLESH, IF YOU'D LIKE. THAT WOULD REALLY PLEASE ME. AND BY THE WAY, I'M GOING TO BE WATCHING YOU ALL THE TIME, EVEN WHEN YOU SLEEP, COOL, EH!" The resident says: "HONEY, QUICK, CALL THE POLICE!"]

God arranging for the execution of his own son to impress humanity about how serious he is in forgiving us for being the descendants of people who ate forbidden fruit is a weird way to go about things. Killing to impress anybody is deplorable and unthinkable to anyone with a shred of morality. If such a person existed today, he would rightly be arrested and put into a psychiatric unit.

> *Why did Jesus have to be executed in a grotesque manner for humans to be freed from sin? Why extract such a heavy toll as death? Why not just forgive? To make us feel SHAME?*

As a few people have pointed out, if Jesus had been executed in our times there would be images of electric chairs in all churches. To my mind, this Christian symbol has the aim of shaming us into obedience and exploiting people's emotions. Implying that believers today are also somehow complicit in this dreadful act of murder is itself a shameful thing to do, especially when it comes to vulnerable children.

SHAMING CHILDREN INTO SUBSERVIENCE IS IMMORAL

> *This image makes me feel ashamed that someone had to die for me. It makes me feel subservient and guilty, as if I owe this person a great debt. This is totally unfair! I had nothing to do with this!*

Using shame as an emotional weapon for control of an adult is bad enough but using it to coerce children into a certain form of behaviour and belief, before they can understand what is happening to them is immoral and wrong.

> *Jesus paid the ultimate sacrifice by dying for our sins, or so we are told... but apparently he is not dead, but alive, so not much of a sacrifice? Why should I feel grateful when he is the all powerful God who I'm told can't die and has complete control over me?*

In fact, he is apparently alive and very well, according to the Church, which somehow makes a mockery of the whole concept of him sacrificing himself for us (for something others did in an obviously mythical event).

The concept of the 'wrath of God' is a common one. This is fearmongering, plain and simple, and this practice should be condemned as a result. Only weak people refer to the threat of suffering to change the behaviour of others, and shouldn't God be above such things?

The notion is bizarre that children must be force-fed religious knowledge before they can develop the ability to think for themselves. This is immoral. As Richard Dawkins rightly points out, there would be uproar if a child were raised as a firm believer in right-wing political thinking from infancy, for example, ensuring that he never had the wherewithal to question this stance.

WHAT'S THE RUSH WITH RELIGION?

[Cartoon: Two adult stick figures labeled "MY PARENTS" speaking to a child]

Parents: THERE HAVE BEEN THOUSANDS OF GODS WORSHIPPED BY HUMANS, NONE OF WHOM HAVE BEEN DISPROVED, BUT WE ARE GOING TO FORCE YOU FROM BIRTH TO BELIEVE IN ONLY ONE OF THEM; OFF TO BAPTISM!

Child: UM, OK... BUT CAN'T I LEARN HOW TO POOH AND TO PEE FIRST?

A child's life should be free from existential concepts, allowing them to focus on important skills for that age (like pooing properly).

RELIGION FORCES CONFORMITY IN LIFE

[Cartoon: Two adult stick figures speaking to a child]

Parents: YOU CAN MAKE YOUR OWN MIND UP ABOUT EVERYTHING ELSE IN LIFE, APART FROM ALL THE REALLY IMPORTANT QUESTIONS IN LIFE, SUCH AS WHERE YOU COME FROM (GOD), WHO MADE YOU (GOD), WHERE YOU ARE GOING AFTER LIFE (GOD'S HOUSE) AND HOW TO BEHAVE EVERY DAY OF YOUR LIFE (OH, AND DON'T BE GAY)

Child: I DID A REALLY BIG POOH AND A WEE AT THE SAME TIME, COOL EH!

AND WHAT'S HIS PROBLEM WITH WOMEN? HE IS SUCH A PATRIARCH

[Cartoon: God figure labeled "GOD"]

God: EVEN THOUGH THE BOYS BREAK THINGS AND MAKE MUCH MORE NOISE THAN THE MORE PLACID GIRLS, I STILL PREFER THEM FOR TRADITION'S SAKE HURRAY!

What type of father would would believe that his daughters are worth less than his sons? This is immoral, cruel, ignorant and misogynistic. It's abundantly clear that, in very general terms, men tend to inflict more violence on society and women tend to be more prominent in roles requiring emotional skills. How can God be so blind to this when he apparently created the two genders himself?

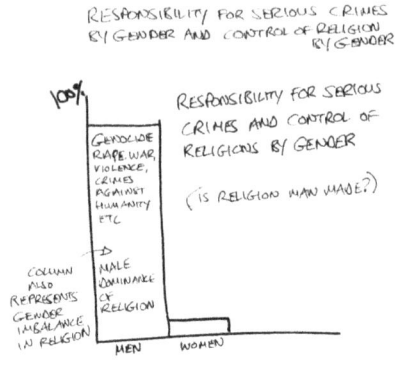

RESPONSIBILITY FOR SERIOUS CRIMES BY GENDER AND CONTROL OF RELIGION BY GENDER

- 100%
- GENOCIDE, RAPE, WAR, VIOLENCE, CRIMES AGAINST HUMANITY ETC
- MALE DOMINANCE OF RELIGION
- RESPONSIBILITY FOR SERIOUS CRIMES AND CONTROL OF RELIGIONS BY GENDER
- (IS RELIGION MAN MADE?)
- COLUMN ALSO REPRESENTS GENDER IMBALANCE IN RELIGION
- MEN / WOMEN

What does the claim that we are made in God's image mean in practice?

WHAT DOES IT MEAN TO SAY THAT GOD IS LIKE MANKIND?

- TESTOSTERONE?
- GENITALS?
- BODY HAIR?
- X+Y CHROMOSOMES?
- NEEDS A FEMALE TO PROCREATE WITH?
- PROBABLY THINKS A LOT ABOUT SPORT AND SEX?
- IS FASCINATED (MOSTLY), AND SOMETIMES BEWILDERED, BY THE FEMALE?

Talking to an invisible being is, let's face it, a bit weird. Sam Harris, an American philosopher and critic of religion, came up with the example below, which sums it all up nicely.

THE PRESIDENT'S HAIR DRYER
(FROM A SAM HARRIS QUOTE)

(A) President G.W. Bush: "I'M TALKING TO GOD THROUGH MY HAIR DRYER" — "IS HE CRAZY?"

(B) President G.W. Bush: "I'M TALKING TO GOD" — "A PRESIDENT WHO PRAYS GETS MY VOTE ALL THE TIME"

WHAT'S THE REAL DIFFERENCE BETWEEN SCENARIOS A AND B?

We are often told that God is full of forgiveness, love, and mercy, but looking at his treatment of his chosen people in the Old Testament (and subsequently) does not bear this out.

THE OLD TESTAMENT....

God: "YOU'LL HAVE A GREAT NATION!" "YOU'LL ALL HAVE A LAND OF MILK AND HONEY!"

GOD OBVIOUSLY PREFERS TOUGH LOVE RATHER THAN COMPASSION AS A PARENT

ABRAHAM → ISAAC → JACOB → EGYPT — FAMINE, ENSLAVEMENT

GOD HELPS THEIR ENEMIES OPPRESS THEM — CONFLICT — BACK TO THE 'PROMISED LAND' — ARDUOUS JOURNEY — MOUNT SINAI — MOSES + THE 10 COMMANDMENTS

↳ CONTINUED HARDSHIP, DESTRUCTION, → 20ᵗʰ CENTURY HOLOCAUST

We are clearly told in the Bible that God is a jealous God, which smacks of real insecurity. Why is he worth worshipping then? How can this be, if he is perfect? And if he is not perfect, then how can he be God?

[Hand-drawn diagram titled "WHY IS GOD SO INSECURE?" showing God in heaven with speech bubbles:]

- "YOU MUST HAVE FAITH IN ME!"
- "YOU MUST BELIEVE IN ME!"
- "(WE HAVE TO PROVE OUR FAITH IN HIM, AND HE TESTS US)"
- "(JUST BEING A REALLY GOOD PERSON ISN'T ENOUGH)"
- "I USED TO BE (STILL AM?) A JEALOUS GOD"
- "THE ONLY WAY TO HEAVEN IS THROUGH JESUS (ME)"
- "I'M GOING TO TEST YOUR DEVOTION TO ME, JUST TO MAKE SURE YOU LOVE ME!"
- "IF YOU BELIEVE IN ME YOU CAN ENTER MY KINGDOM AND PRAISE ME FOR EVER!"
- "I DEMAND ATTENTION! YOU SHOULD REMIND ME EVERY SUNDAY (AT LEAST) THAT YOU FOLLOW AND BELIEVE IN AND LOVE ME!"
- "AND YOU HAVE TO DO THE WORK, PERSUADING OTHERS HOW GREAT AND WORTHY I AM."
- "AND I DEMAND RESPECT"

In contradictory behaviour, he is also very shy, for a jealous God. If he wants everyone to worship and praise him regularly to subdue his jealousy, appearing in person might be a good idea.

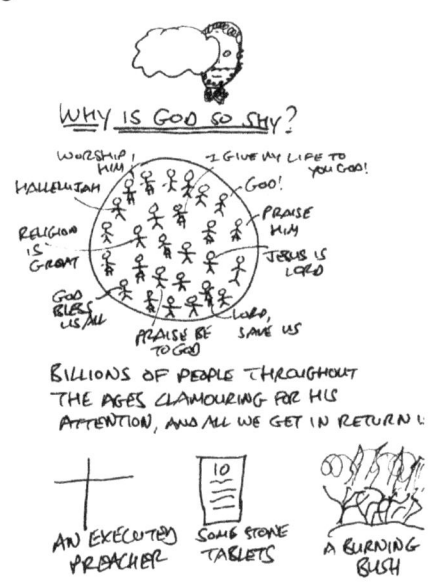

[Hand-drawn diagram titled "WHY IS GOD SO SHY?" showing a crowd of stick figures around "GOD" with phrases:]

- "WORSHIP HIM"
- "HALLELUJAH"
- "I GIVE MY LIFE TO YOU GOD!"
- "PRAISE HIM"
- "RELIGION IS GREAT"
- "JESUS IS LORD"
- "GOD BLESS US ALL"
- "PRAISE BE TO GOD"
- "LORD, SAVE US"

BILLIONS OF PEOPLE THROUGHOUT THE AGES CLAMOURING FOR HIS ATTENTION, AND ALL WE GET IN RETURN:

- AN EXECUTED PREACHER
- SOME STONE TABLETS
- A BURNING BUSH

And on a related note, why did God wait for well over 100,000 years as our species struggled along before having himself crucified on earth?

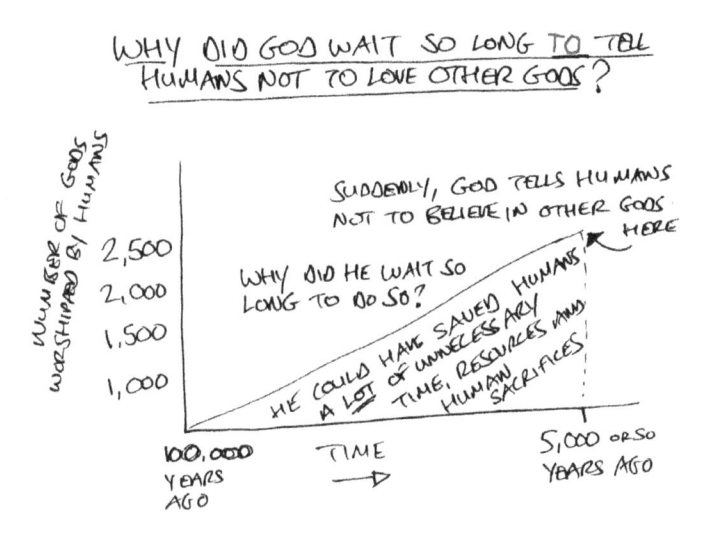

WHY DID GOD WAIT SO LONG TO TELL HUMANS NOT TO LOVE OTHER GODS?

[Hand-drawn graph with y-axis labeled "NUMBER OF GODS WORSHIPPED BY HUMANS" with values 1,000, 1,500, 2,000, 2,500; x-axis labeled "TIME" from "100,000 YEARS AGO" to "5,000 OR SO YEARS AGO". Annotations on the graph: "SUDDENLY, GOD TELLS HUMANS NOT TO BELIEVE IN OTHER GODS HERE", "WHY DID HE WAIT SO LONG TO DO SO?", "HE COULD HAVE SAVED HUMANS A LOT OF UNNECESSARY TIME, RESOURCES AND HUMAN SACRIFICES!"]

5. Which bit of being gay is a sin?

Turning to a more specific issue now, that of the Church's teaching on homosexuality and those infamous lines in Leviticus: "If a man lies with a male as with a woman, both of them have committed an abomination; they shall surely be put to death; their blood is upon them." – Chapter 20, verse 13. The Church has a bizarre focus on homosexuality rather than on other sins identified in the Old Testament (witchcraft, blasphemy, working on the Sabbath, etc.), but it's never been clear to me which bit of being gay is wrong. Any clarity from Catholics on this topic would be appreciated! (One should also mention in this context the Catholic Church's damaging views on contraception and abortion, especially as it relates to the spread of AIDS in some of the world's most impoverished places, the growing risks of overpopulation, as well as the crippling effect on women's ability to work their way out of poverty.)

WHICH BIT OF BEING GAY IS SO WRONG?

- JUST BEING GAY?
- JUST LOVING ANOTHER PERSON?
- HOW CAN ANOTHER LOVING FAITHFULLY PERSON COMPASSIONATELY AND BE IN ANY WAY WRONG?
- HOLDING HANDS?
- KISSING?
- TOUCHING A MAN'S WILLY? PUTTING YOUR WILLY NEAR A MAN'S BOTTOM / IN HIS BOTTOM REALLY QUICKLY / LONGER?
- KISSING HIS WILLY ONCE? PUTTING IT IN YOUR MOUTH FOR A DARE? LICKING HIS WILLY IF YOU AREN'T GAY, JUST CURIOUS?
- OR IS IT ALL TO DO WITH MAKING A MAN EJACULATE? IF SO, WHY? GUIDANCE, PLEASE!!
- WHAT IF TWO HETEROSEXUAL MEN DECIDE TO HAVE ANAL SEX FOR CHARITY, WITH PROCEEDS GOING TO GOOD CAUSES?
- IS LESBIANISM WRONG? IF SO, WHICH FORMS?
- HOW CAN IT BE UNNATURAL WHEN SO MANY OTHER ANIMALS DO IT?

6. What makes Jesus' teachings automatically moral?

As the late Christopher Hitchens used to point out, even if we do accept all the extraordinary claims about God and Jesus, it still doesn't mean that Jesus' preaching should be regarded as moral truths.

EVEN IF YOU BELIEVE ALL OF THIS...

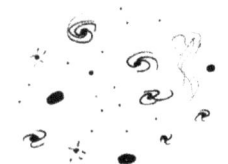

EVEN IF YOU BELIEVE THERE IS A CREATOR OF THIS POSSIBLY INFINITE UNIVERSE, YOU THEN HAVE TO BELIEVE HE IS AWARE

OF LITTLE OLD US, ON A MOTE OF UNIVERSAL DUST

A TINY DROP IN THE VAST OCEAN OF SPACE AND TIME, AND THAT HE KNOWS ALL OF US (7,000,000,000...) HI!! HOLA! GRÜSS GOTT!

THIS IS VERY TEDIOUS

GOD THE POLICEMAN

AND THAT HE/IT SPENDS HIS WHOLE TIME SCRUTINISING US LIKE CHILDREN

7 BILLION OF US SCUTTLING AROUND LIKE BACTERIA ON A PIECE OF MUD

EVEN THOUGH HE HAS AN INFINITE AMOUNT OF SPACE AND TIME TO SURVEY

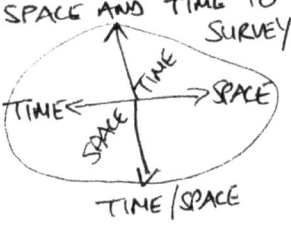

TIME / SPACE

AS WELL AS OTHER POSSIBLE UNIVERSES

MULTIVERSE?

YOU ALSO HAVE TO BELIEVE HE CARES VERY MUCH ABOUT IF WE SAY THE RIGHT WORDS, LOVE THE WRONG PEOPLE, EAT THE WRONG FOOD

FOR GOD'S SAKE!

AND WHETHER WE CALL HIM EVERY DAY, AND VISIT HIM AT LEAST 60 TIMES A YEAR

[Drawing of a church with a thought bubble showing God: "MRS EVANS ONLY WENT TO CHURCH TO SEE ME 59 TIMES LAST YEAR, NOT ENOUGH!"]

AND THAT WE ALL HAVE A REPLICA OF HIS DEAD BUT ALIVE MUTILATED SON IN HIS MOMENT OF TOTAL HUMILIATION STUCK TO OUR WALLS ALL THE TIME

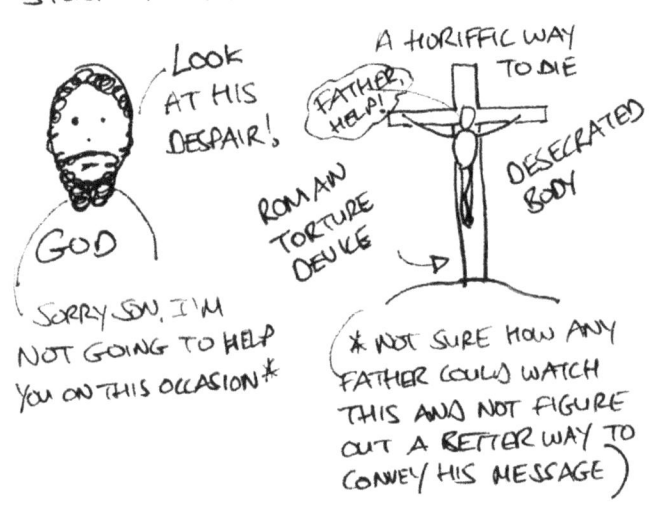

[Drawing of God's face labeled "LOOK AT HIS DESPAIR!" and "GOD" — "SORRY SON, I'M NOT GOING TO HELP YOU ON THIS OCCASION"]*

[Drawing of crucifix with labels: "A HORIFFIC WAY TO DIE", "FATHER, HELP!", "ROMAN TORTURE DEVICE", "DESECRATED BODY"]

(* NOT SURE HOW ANY FATHER COULD WATCH THIS AND NOT FIGURE OUT A BETTER WAY TO CONVEY HIS MESSAGE)

AND THAT HE WANTS US TO CANNIBALISE HIS SON'S BODY EVERY WEEK...

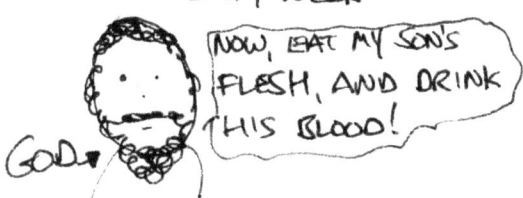

GOD → "NOW, EAT MY SON'S FLESH, AND DRINK THIS BLOOD!"

"THE BODY OF CHRIST" — "AMEN"

CHURCH ON A SUNDAY

EVEN IF YOU BELIEVE ALL OF THIS YOU STILL HAVE TO PROVE THAT HIS REPORTED TEACHINGS ARE **MORAL**

THE 10 COMMANDMENTS
- THOU SHALT HAVE NO OTHER GODS BEFORE ME (?!)
- DON'T EVEN THINK ABOUT FINDING A WOMAN ATTRACTIVE (?!)

JESUS
- LEAVE YOUR FAMILY, NOW!
- I'LL TAKE AWAY YOUR RESPONSIBILITY FOR YOUR ACTIONS (?.!)
- LOVE YOUR ENEMIES

Where is the link between doing miracles and being an amazing moral philosopher? Anyway, why not call events such as walking on water 'sorcery', 'wizardry' or 'witchcraft'?

7. God couldn't organise a booze-up in a brewery – how God made a mess of his grand plan

If God is so great, and perfect, and omnipresent, and all-knowing, why did he make such a mess of creating the world and humanity in the first place (necessitating all those violent interventions of his in the Old Testament)?

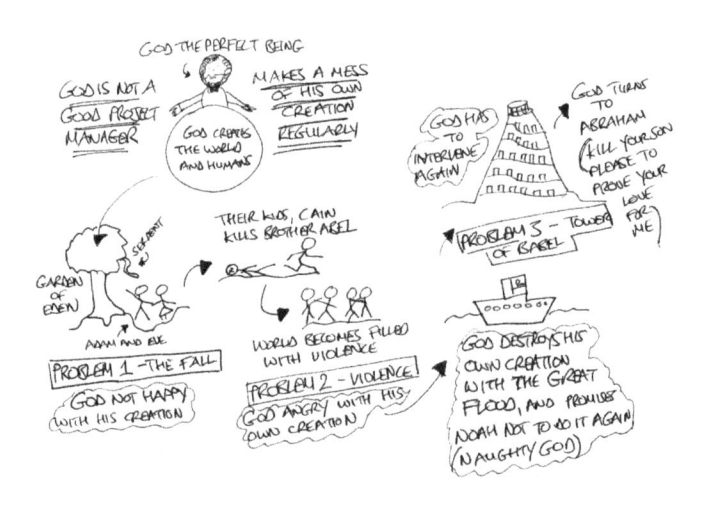

And the way the supposed greatest event of all time – the birth, life and death of Jesus Christ – was organised, implemented and not followed up, is lamentable.

PRE-DEPLOYMENT PLANNING MEETING

GOD: I'm/we are glad to agree with myself/ourselves on the following strategy for the biggest announcement ever!

THE HOLY GHOST

BABY JESUS

① LET'S GO TO A RELATIVELY REMOTE PART OF THE WORLD, CONFUSE OURSELVES WITH AN EXISTING RELIGION AND NOT MOVE MORE THAN 100 KM FROM OUR STARTING POINT.

② HAVE YOU GOT A PEN? WHAT'S A PEN? OUR TARGET AUDIENCE IS UNEDUCATED, ILLITERATE, SEMI-NOMADIC PEASANTS WHO HAVE NO INFLUENCE OR SOCIAL OR ECONOMIC POWER TO HELP SPREAD THE WORD

③ WRITING IS FOR LOSERS. LET'S NOT WRITE ANYTHING DOWN, AND MAKE SURE NO-ONE ELSE DOES EITHER. THERE'S NO POINT BECAUSE...

④ JUDGMENT DAY — OUR KEY MESSAGE IS THAT THE KINGDOM OF GOD IS AT HAND — DROP EVERYTHING, LEAVE YOUR FAMILY, REPENT AND FOLLOW ME BECAUSE JUDGMENT DAY IS COMING VERY SOON!

⑤ TO GRAB THEIR ATTENTION AND TO SHOW HOW MUCH I/WE LOVE PEOPLE LET'S KILL ME/YOU IN A GROTESQUE AND BARBARIC MANNER IN A PUBLIC AND HUMILIATING MANNER, AND THEN BLAME EVERYONE IN THE PAST AND FUTURE FOR FORCING ME/US TO DO THIS BECAUSE I LET THAT SNAKE CONVINCE MY FIRST TWO PERSONS TO EAT THAT APPLE.

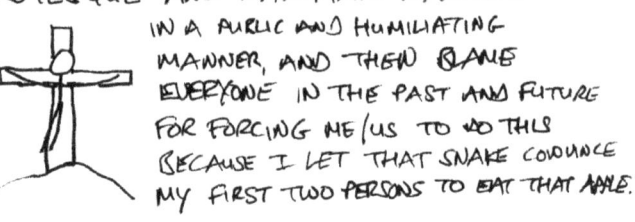

⑥ LET'S THEN SIT BACK AND RELAX FOR THE NEXT 2,000 YEARS AND WATCH THE CHAOS UNFOLD!

DON'T FORGET TO WORSHIP ME/US ALL THE TIME!

JESUS GOD HOLY SPIRIT

HEAVEN

THE EARTH → RELIGIOUS WARS / SCHISMS IN CHRISTIANITY / THE CRUSADES / CONTINUED CONFUSION / BLOODLETTING

BUT HE'S 2,000 YEARS LATE

IT'S A METAPHOR

"SHOULDN'T WE CLARIFY THINGS AND HELP OUT A BIT?"

"I GAVE A FEW UNRECORDED, RATHER VAGUE SPEECHES IN THE DESERT. WHAT MORE DO THEY WANT? AND IT'S ALL THEIR FAULT ANYWAY - THEY SHOULDN'T HAVE EATEN THAT APPLE! YOU/I'M ALWAYS GOING ON ABOUT APPLES - WHAT'S WITH YOU/ME?"

⑦ AND TO CAP IT ALL OFF, LET'S MAKE SURE THE SOURCE MATERIAL FOR THE GOSPELS GETS LOST - NO POINT MAKING IT TOO EASY FOR THEM...

Q → BIN

It appears then that God flunked his big announcement.

8. And his promotional tactics would be banned these days…

The Catholic Church, it appears, would fail basic advertising standards in the United Kingdom (and likely in other developed countries), notably the UK's Advertising Standards Authority (ASA) code, 03 Misleading advertising, point 3.7:

Before distributing or submitting a marketing communication for publication, marketers must hold documentary evidence to prove claims that consumers are likely to regard as objective and that are capable of objective substantiation. The ASA may regard claims as misleading in the absence of adequate substantiation.

and point 3.8:

Claims for the content of non-fiction publications should not exaggerate the value, accuracy, scientific validity or practical usefulness of the product. Marketers must ensure that claims that have not been independently substantiated but are based merely on the content of a publication do not mislead consumers.

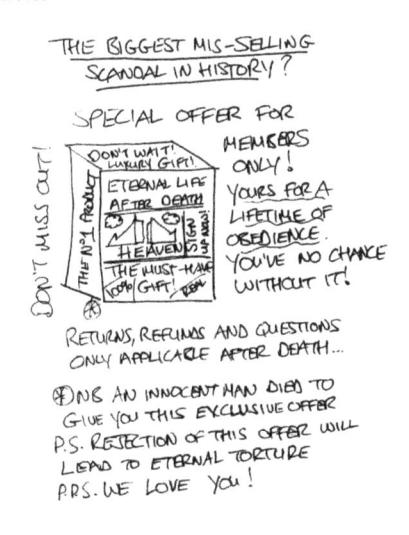

THE BIGGEST MIS-SELLING SCANDAL IN HISTORY?

SPECIAL OFFER FOR MEMBERS ONLY!
DON'T WAIT! LUXURY GIFT!
ETERNAL LIFE AFTER DEATH
HEAVEN
THE MUST-HAVE GIFT!
YOURS FOR A LIFETIME OF OBEDIENCE. YOU'VE NO CHANCE WITHOUT IT!
DON'T MISS OUT!
THE N°1 PRODUCT

RETURNS, REFUNDS AND QUESTIONS ONLY APPLICABLE AFTER DEATH…

NB AN INNOCENT MAN DIED TO GIVE YOU THIS EXCLUSIVE OFFER
P.S. REJECTION OF THIS OFFER WILL LEAD TO ETERNAL TORTURE
P.P.S. WE LOVE YOU!

The Church's message involves targeting children before they can comprehend what they are being told. This falls foul of the ASA's code for advertising to children, point 5.1:

Marketing communications addressed to, targeted directly at or featuring children must contain nothing that is likely to result in their physical, mental or moral harm:

And especially point 5.2:

Marketing communications addressed to, targeted directly at or featuring children must not exploit their credulity, loyalty, vulnerability or lack of experience.

And subsequent points:

5.2.1 children must not be made to feel inferior or unpopular for not buying the advertised product.

5.2.2 children must not be made to feel that they are lacking in courage, duty or loyalty if they do not buy or do not encourage others to buy a product.

5.2.3 it must be made easy for children to judge the size, characteristics and performance of advertised products and to distinguish between real-life situations and fantasy.

If chocolate and fast-food manufacturers have to abide by these common-sense rules, why shouldn't a multinational organisation as big as the Catholic Church with its huge influence and resources?

A GREAT SALES TACTIC

- You have a big problem! And only the church can fix it
- Ok, I'm sold, scared and very credulous, help me!

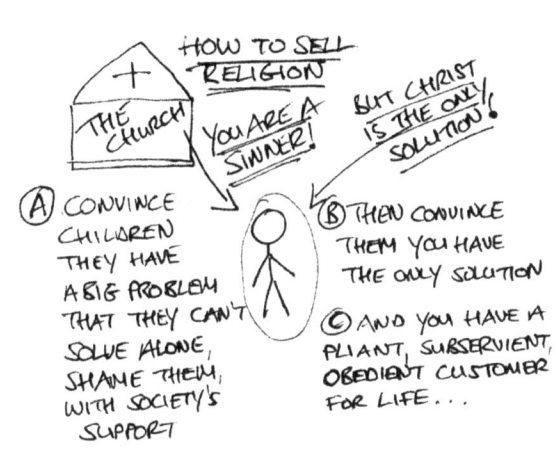

HOW TO SELL RELIGION

THE CHURCH — "YOU ARE A SINNER!" — "BUT CHRIST IS THE ONLY SOLUTION!"

(A) Convince children they have a big problem that they can't solve alone, shame them, with society's support

(B) Then convince them you have the only solution

(C) And you have a pliant, subservient, obedient customer for life...

I felt frustrated when I realised I had been CONNED
(but now it feels great to be free of it)

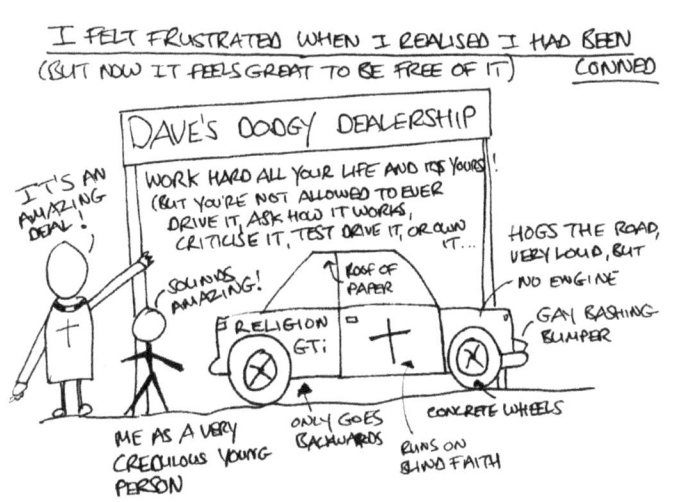

DAVE'S DODGY DEALERSHIP

Work hard all your life and it's yours! (but you're not allowed to ever drive it, ask how it works, criticise it, test drive it, or own it...)

- It's an amazing deal!
- Sounds amazing!
- Roof of paper
- Religion GTi
- Hogs the road, very loud, but no engine
- Gay bashing bumper
- Me as a very credulous young person
- Only goes backwards
- Runs on blind faith
- Concrete wheels

9. God deserves to be 'unfriended'

MAYBE GOD JUST DOESN'T WANT US TO CONTACT HIM?

09:04 — YOU HAVE SEVEN BILLION MISSED CALLS AND ONE TRILLION UNANSWERED MESSAGES. GOD'S PHONE. PRESS HOME TO UNLOCK.

IF A FRIEND OR PARENT NEVER RETURNED A PHONE CALL OF MINE, I WOULD REGARD THEM AS <u>RUDE AND ARROGANT</u>

OUT OF A SENSE OF SELF RESPECT, PERHAPS WE SHOULD TRY, JUST FOR A BIT, TO UNFRIEND HIM?

GOD ▼ — UNFRIEND — CLICK

If God wants us to get back in touch, or is concerned about being 'unfriended' by his children, then he could just ask.

A solution to the Middle East peace process

I propose a similar approach to the Middle East peace process. The problem there seems to be about the competing religious claims bound up in the region, above other issues. I think we should just send a memo to God asking what he thinks the answer is, with a silence procedure of, say, six months. If we have not heard from him by the end of this period, we should proclaim him as disinterested and solve the problem on purely secular terms.

10. God is like any other emotionally disengaged father

The comparisons between an emotionally disengaged father and God seem to be numerous. To my mind, he fails his claim to fatherhood in basic ways.

GOD IS JUST LIKE A PRETTY POOR FATHER

GOD	vs	ABSENT FATHER
RESPECTED JUST BECAUSE THEY ARE A FATHER FIGURE		DITTO
THEY NEED TO BE REMINDED (PRAYERS) ABOUT IMPORTANT THINGS THEY SHOULD BE PROACTIVE ABOUT		DITTO
THEY ALMOST NEVER MAKE THE EFFORT TO PROPERLY ENGAGE WITH THEIR KIDS		DITTO
YOU FEEL YOU OWE THEM JUST BECAUSE THEY'RE YOUR FATHER		DITTO
THEY DON'T GIVE WOMEN THE RESPECT THEY DESERVE		DITTO
THEY GENERALLY DON'T SEEM THAT INTERESTED IN YOU		DITTO
NO AMOUNT OF PLEADING WILL EVER CHANGE THEM		DITTO
YOU NEVER QUITE UNDERSTAND WHAT MAKES THEM TICK		DITTO

IT'S ALWAYS YOU WHO HAS TO MAKE THE EFFORT TO VISIT THEM, AND THEN THEY RARELY SAY MUCH	DITTO
AS A CHILD THEY KIND OF SCARE YOU AS THEY APPEAR SO POWERFUL	DITTO
THEY DEMAND OBEDIENCE, JUST BECAUSE THEY SAY SO	DITTO
ALL THEY HAVE TO OFFER IS BREAD AND WINE	DITTO
THEY SEEM STRONG AND POWERFUL BUT THEY ACTUALLY NEED A LOT OF PRAISE AND ATTENTION	DITTO
THEY OFTEN LIVE ALONE (WHERE IS GOD'S WIFE?)	DITTO
THEY ARE ALOOF, DISTANT AND HARD TO PIN DOWN	DITTO
YOU MAY HAVE TO MOVE BACK IN WITH THEM AT SOME POINT	DITTO

THEY ALWAYS CLAIM THEY LOVE YOU; YOU ARE NEVER QUITE SURE IF THIS IS TRUE   DITTO

SEX IS NEVER A TOPIC FOR DISCUSSION WITH THEM   DITTO

THEY LOVE HAVING AN IMPORTANT POSITION LIKE HEAD OF A CHURCH / GOLF CLUB   DITTO

THEY LOVE SETTING OUT RULES AND REGULATIONS   DITTO

YOU SOMETIMES WISH THEY WOULDN'T TAKE THEMSELVES TOO SERIOUSLY   DITTO

THEY REALLY HATE IT IF THEIR SON IS GAY   DITTO

YOU HEARD THAT IN THE PAST THEY HELD VERY RIGHT WING, FASCIST VIEWS, WERE JEALOUS AND GOT VIOLENTLY ANGRY   DITTO

11. Where did all this belief stuff come from anyway?

After trying to sort out my religious head stuffed full of Catholicism, I started to wonder where our species' attraction to religion came from originally. After a little bit of research, a simple and plausible explanation started to materialise.

OUR PARANOID, PATTERN SEEKING ANCESTORS

I SURVIVE BY CONSTANTLY TRYING TO MAKE CONNECTIONS AND NOTICE PATTERNS IN MY ENVIRONMENT; COMBINED WITH A VERY CAUTIOUS ATTITUDE, THIS KEEPS ME ALIVE. I TEACH MY KIDS TO LOOK FOR MEANING IN OUR ENVIRONMENT, INCLUDING TO INANIMATE THINGS SUCH AS WIND, STORMS ETC.

OUR/MY GREAT-GREAT-GREAT (× 10,000) GRANDFATHER

I'M SCARED AND I DESPERATELY WANT TO FEEL SECURE SO I'LL TELL SOME COMFORTING STORIES...

PRE-HISTORIC CAVEMAN

HEAVEN

We must go somewhere after we die, and it must be up in the sky...

It's not fair that bad people get away with bad things so they must be punished. The place they go to must be under the ground, like the inside of a volcano

HELL — LAVA — FIRE

GOD

There must be someone in charge of these places, a good man and a bad man

They must both be nearby as the sun goes around the earth and we are all that exists...

THE DEVIL

HOW THE IDEA OF GOD CAME TO BE

He must also be invisible as I can't see him

It must be a bigger version of me, an amazing, powerful man

I must be the reason all this around me exists – it was made for me

Who made all of this around me?

I must be grateful for this and be submissive to this amazing, invisible me

I must be so special to him, otherwise he would not have done so much creating

WE ARE ALSO PATTERN SEEKING HUNTER GATHERERS CONSTANTLY INTERPRETING EVENTS IN ORDER TO SURVIVE

☀ + ☁ = GROWTH AND FOOD SOURCES

BUFFALO + SEASONS = ANNUAL MIGRATIONS

STORMS + VOLCANOES = BIG MAN IN SKY UNHAPPY

THE AMAZING ME!

KNOWING THAT THERE MUST BE A BIG, INCREDIBLE VERSION OF ME IN THE SKY, WHO IS INVISIBLE, IS VERY REASSURING. HE MUST ALSO LOOK AFTER ALL THE PEOPLE WHO STOP LIVING. WE MUST BE REALLY NICE TO HIM!

RELIGION — OUR FIRST ATTEMPT TO EXPLAIN THE INEXPLICABLE

— WINDS, GODS, THE UNDEAD
THE STARS, SACRIFICE
THE SEASONS, THE NEXT LIFE

WE LIKE SITTING AROUND OUR FIRE TELLING STORIES
WHOEVER TELLS THE BEST, MOST WONDERFUL STORIES
EARNS A LOT OF RESPECT, AND IS GREATLY ADMIRED

GLACIERS AND MOUNTAINS
STORMS, LIGHTNING AND THUNDER
VOLCANO

SHARING AND BELIEVING IN OUR GREAT
STORIES GIVES US A SENSE OF BELONGING,
A SENSE OF COMMUNITY, A COMMON NARRATIVE,
AND A SENSE OF CONTROL

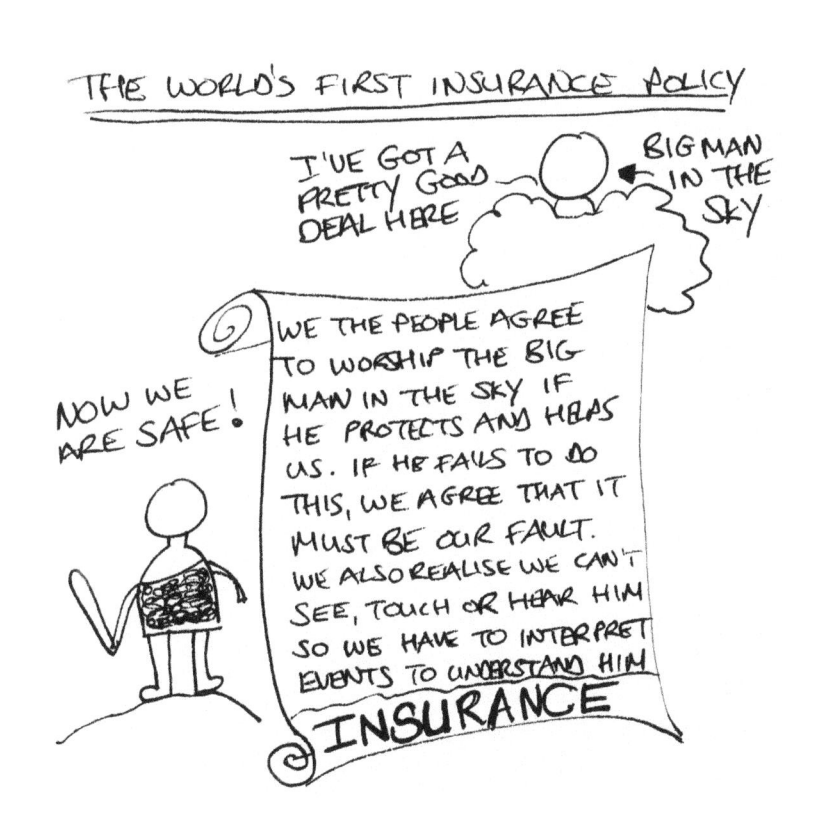

WE ARE A NATURALLY CURIOUS SPECIES, AND WHEN CATASTROPHES OCCUR, LIKE PLAGUES, WE CRAVE ANSWERS...

"THE BIG MAN IN THE SKY MUST BE VERY ANGRY WITH US"

DEAD BODIES, PLAGUE VICTIMS

THE WORLD'S FIRST INSURANCE POLICY

"I'VE GOT A PRETTY GOOD DEAL HERE"

BIG MAN IN THE SKY

"NOW WE ARE SAFE!"

WE THE PEOPLE AGREE TO WORSHIP THE BIG MAN IN THE SKY, IF HE PROTECTS AND HELPS US. IF HE FAILS TO DO THIS, WE AGREE THAT IT MUST BE OUR FAULT. WE ALSO REALISE WE CAN'T SEE, TOUCH OR HEAR HIM SO WE HAVE TO INTERPRET EVENTS TO UNDERSTAND HIM

INSURANCE

THIS LED TO THE WORSHIP OF THOUSANDS OF DIFFERENT DEITIES DOWN THE AGES, OF ALL DIFFERENT SHAPES AND SIZES...

SUN GODS

SKY GODS

ANIMAL TYPE GODS

GODS OF THE UNDERWORLD

GODS OF THUNDER, LIGHTNING, WIND, RAIN ETC

TRIAD GODS

PEOPLE CONSIDERED AS DEITIES

...AND THEY NUMBER IN THE THOUSANDS

THERE HAVE BEEN MANY KINGS
OF THE GODS, WHO CAN ALL

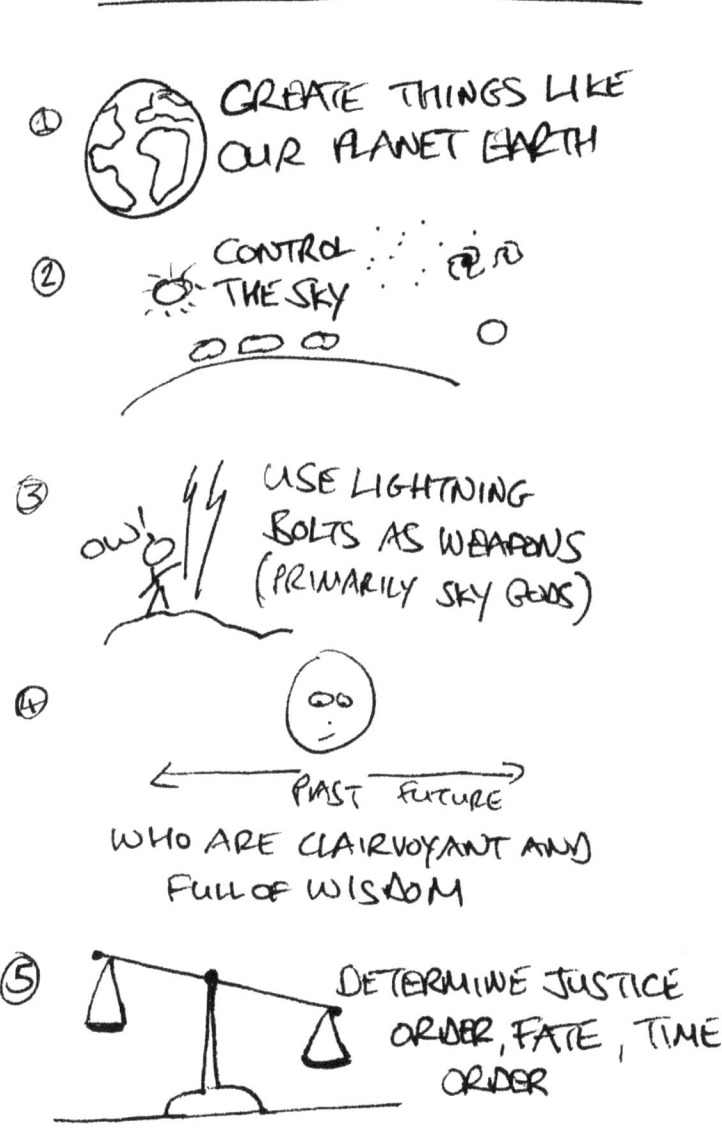

① CREATE THINGS LIKE OUR PLANET EARTH

② CONTROL THE SKY

③ USE LIGHTNING BOLTS AS WEAPONS (PRIMARILY SKY GODS)

ow!

④ PAST ← → FUTURE

WHO ARE CLAIRVOYANT AND FULL OF WISDOM

⑤ DETERMINE JUSTICE ORDER, FATE, TIME ORDER

CHARACTERISTICS OF SOME OF THESE PEOPLE REGARDED AS DEITIES INCLUDE:

- VIRGIN BIRTHS
- BIRTHS MARKED BY A STAR
- WISE MEN
- FIGHTING EVIL FORCES
- DYING ON A HILL
- APPEARING AFTER DEATH
- ASCENDING INTO HEAVEN

Luckily for followers of early Christianity, Roman Emperor Constantine became a great patron of the religion, which helped its ~~spread~~ hugely

Hurray!

And he helped codify the faith at the First Council of Nicea in CE 325

Christianity arguably survived as a religion due to enforcement of unitary belief

100% — Level of importance of influence

Enforcement of belief by Roman Empire in Christianity on its population

↑ Potency of Jesus's message

12. A flimsy edifice? Central accounts in the Bible appear to be based on myth and legend

Religion at first glance looks so solid and robust. The amazing churches, the billion plus followers, the thousand-year-old traditions, the music, art and architecture it has inspired and its moral influence. However, when I tried to look at its bedrock foundations, from which all its doctrine and teachings stems, it turned out to be flimsy in my eyes.

It's amazing how little I knew about the Bible, despite years of education in religious schools, studying theology for A-level and being a practising Catholic for so many years. I just took it for granted that it was all true, like many other people I guess. The fact that I grew up within a Christian culture just made the Bible into a de facto book of truth, a fact that was not even worth questioning as it was so embedded in society.

I realised the Bible was not without fundamental flaws if regarded as the ultimate book of truth and the word of God.

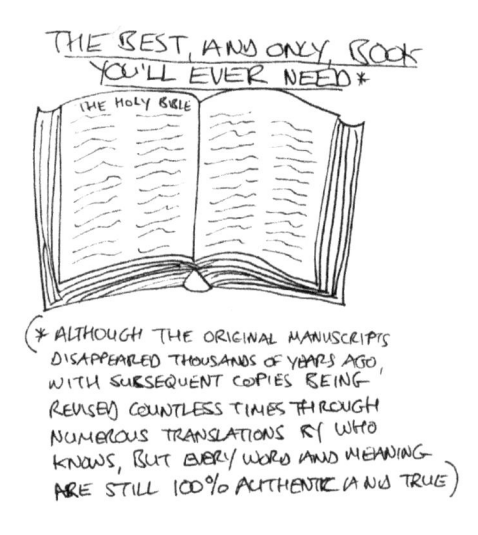

[Hand-drawn illustration of an open Bible labelled "THE HOLY BIBLE" with the caption above: "THE BEST, AND ONLY, BOOK YOU'LL EVER NEED" and below: "(* ALTHOUGH THE ORIGINAL MANUSCRIPTS DISAPPEARED THOUSANDS OF YEARS AGO, WITH SUBSEQUENT COPIES BEING REVISED COUNTLESS TIMES THROUGH NUMEROUS TRANSLATIONS BY WHO KNOWS, BUT EVERY WORD AND MEANING ARE STILL 100% AUTHENTIC AND TRUE)"]*

After reading a fair bit about it I realised that it had some very peculiar accounts in it, especially in the Old Testament.

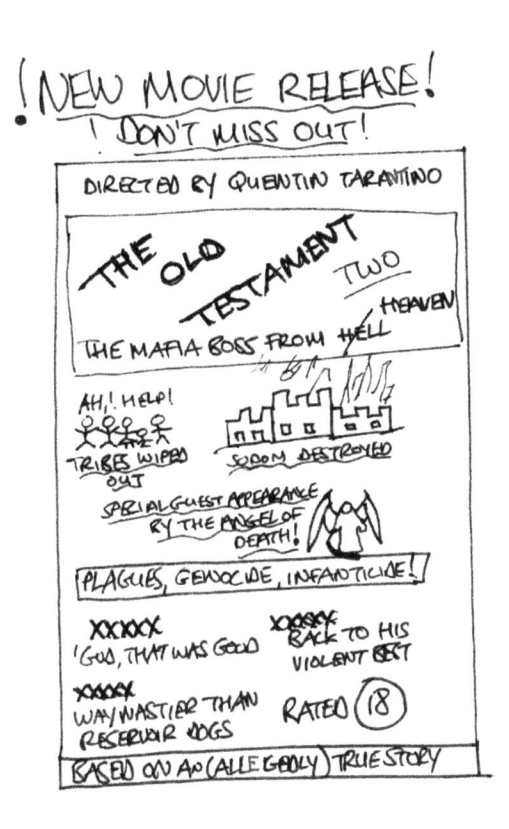

One thing I was only vaguely aware of is the connection between first Judaism, then Christianity and then Islam. It's a bit like a TV show that has spin-off sequels, like *Breaking Bad* and *Better Call Saul*, meaning they all stem from the same original characters. In this case of religion, the founding character is Abraham. He's important as he is the first person identified in Judaism whom God chose, contacted and agreed a covenant (or contract) with, promising that he would be blessed and that his ancestors would inherit the Promised Land. This was followed in Judaism by other covenants between God and chosen individuals such as Jacob (Abraham's grandson, with his famous ladder), Moses (and the ten commandments) and later David. In addition, there is God's covenant with Noah (which covers all mankind rather than just the descendants of Abraham). Christians of course believe in all these Old Testament accounts and in addition believe that the arrival of Jesus marked a new covenant with God, for all people. Islam also accepts that God revealed himself to Abraham and regards him as a prophet and messenger from God, as part of a chain of prophets from Adam culminating in Muhammad. Islam also grants special status to Jesus and Mary.

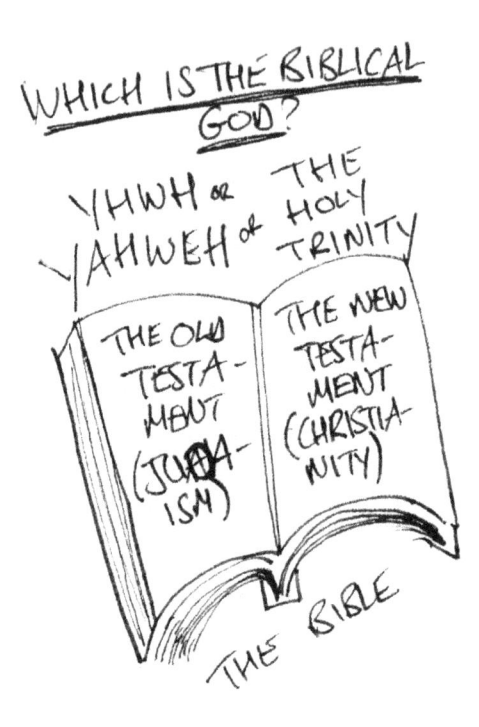

WHICH IS THE BIBLICAL GOD?
YHWH or YAHWEH or THE HOLY TRINITY
THE OLD TESTAMENT (JUDAISM) / THE NEW TESTAMENT (CHRISTIANITY)
THE BIBLE

If Abraham, and subsequent key characters for all three religions, is so important, you would think that there is overwhelming and convincing evidence for his existence. Not having this would necessarily call into question all subsequent events and religious claims. Yet the evidence for the existence of a specific person we now regard as Abraham is in no way overwhelming.

THE KEYSTONE OF JUDAISM, ABRAHAM'S VISION OF GOD, FOLLOWED BY JACOB'S DREAM

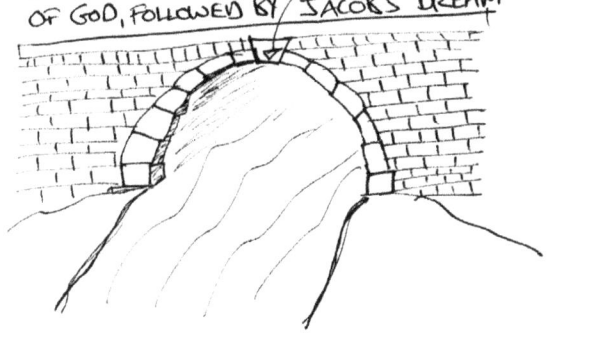

[Illustration: a stone archway with a keystone]

[Illustration: a person sleeping with a thought bubble showing "HEAVEN", "JACOB'S LADDER", angels on a ladder, and God saying "JACOB, YOU ARE THE BLESSED ONE AND THIS LAND IS NOW YOURS"]

ALL 3 ABRAHAMIC RELIGIONS SEEM TO REST ON THIS ONE DREAM

GOD APPEARING TO JACOB IN A DREAM

IF WE DON'T BELIEVE THESE DAYS THAT DREAMS INCLUDE MESSAGES FROM GOD, WHY SHOULD WE GIVE LEGITIMACY TO STORIES ABOUT DREAMS FROM UP TO 3,000 YEARS AGO?

RELIGIONS ARE BASED ON LEGENDS

MADE FROM 100% RECYCLED ORAL TRADITIONS FROM DIFFERING SOURCES OVER CENTURIES

- THE FATHER OF JUDAISM
- CATHOLICISM'S FATHER IN FAITH
- A PROPHET AND PATRIARCH IN ISLAM

ALMOST CERTAINLY NEVER EXISTED AS A SPECIFIC HISTORICAL INDIVIDUAL

HAD A VISION OF GOD RESULTING IN A COVENANT BETWEEN THEM DESPITE NOT BEING A REAL PERSON

YET RESPECTED BY JUDAISM, CHRISTIANITY AND ISLAM

ABRAHAM

THE MOST IMPORTANT PERSON NEVER TO HAVE EXISTED!

Even if there was overwhelming evidence of Abraham's existence, it's still a big leap to believe that God spoke to him and made a covenant with him. Even if this is plausible, the questions continue. How do we know that this supernatural being contacting Abraham was trustworthy and not just some kind of supernatural troublemaker who wanted to sow a bit of confusion? What if it was even an evil form of supernatural being who wanted to sow division among the peoples at the time? Even if it was a good-natured supernatural being, what gives him the right to exclude from the covenant other people existing in the region at the time, and subsequently? There is overwhelming evidence for the evolution of the universe and our planet, so if God didn't create the world, what gives him the right to grant a part of it in perpetuity to a certain group of people and not others? If my father said to me, "you will inherit all my possessions, including my house, none of which will go to your two siblings"; I would reject such a proposal as manifestly unfair and unjust. Shouldn't this also apply to any covenant where a supernatural being is giving away what isn't his to an arbitrary group of people above all others? One can't claim that the descendants of Abraham were in any way more deserving of such a gift as this would be a hugely discriminatory step. And yet civilisation today, thousands of years later, is still willing to accept this covenant as a deal that should somehow be respected. And of course, this approach applies to all religions where an apparent supernatural being grants advantages to one set of people to the detriment of others on apparent arbitrary grounds.

Religion now seems to me to be like a big *Angry Birds* structure. If you throw some considered, knowledgeable answers at it, the whole edifice starts looking very unstable.

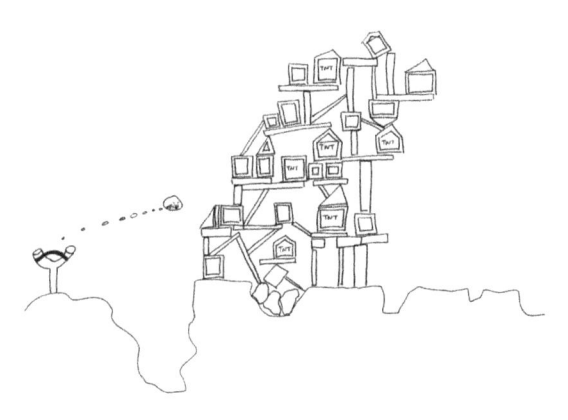

The image of a precariously balanced house of cards also comes to mind.

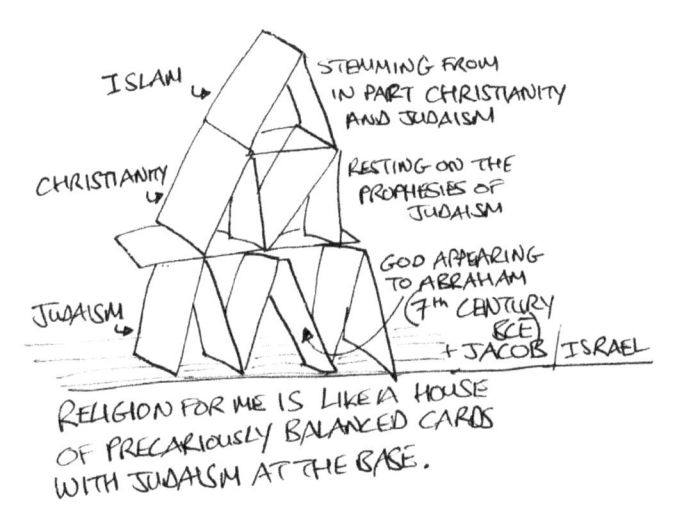

These purported events also depend heavily on visions and dreams.

AUDITORY HALLUCINATIONS OFTEN OCCUR IF YOU ARE COMPLETELY ISOLATED FOR A FEW DAYS

I'M STARTING TO HEAR VOICES AND SOUNDS - WEIRD!

ME, IN A CAVE COMPLETELY ALONE FOR 3 DAYS...

Dreams and apparent visions are commonplace.

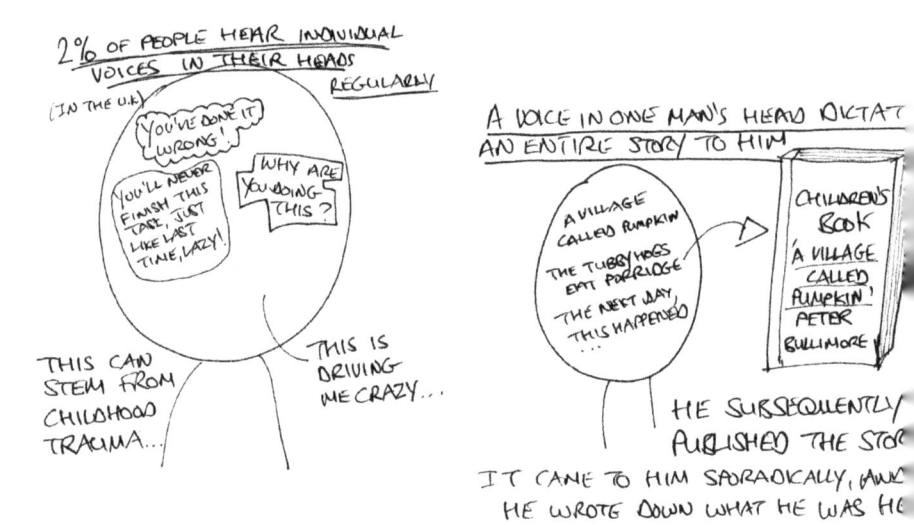

2% OF PEOPLE HEAR INDIVIDUAL VOICES IN THEIR HEADS REGULARLY (IN THE U.K.)

YOU'VE DONE IT WRONG!

YOU'LL NEVER FINISH THIS TASK, JUST LIKE LAST TIME, LAZY!

WHY ARE YOU DOING THIS?

THIS CAN STEM FROM CHILDHOOD TRAUMA...

THIS IS DRIVING ME CRAZY...

A VOICE IN ONE MAN'S HEAD DICTATED AN ENTIRE STORY TO HIM

A VILLAGE CALLED PUMPKIN
THE TUBBYHOGS EAT PORRIDGE
THE NEXT DAY, THIS HAPPENED...

CHILDREN'S BOOK
A VILLAGE CALLED PUMPKIN
PETER BULLIMORE

HE SUBSEQUENTLY PUBLISHED THE STORY
IT CAME TO HIM SPORADICALLY, AND HE WROTE DOWN WHAT HE WAS HE

Accounts in the Bible come from primitive times thousands of years ago.

Religion is based on the alleged dreams and visions of ancient characters whose existence as characterised in the Bible is difficult to ascertain. It is hard to avoid the conclusion therefore that religion has very shaky foundations indeed, and certainly foundations too weak to base the workings and politics of whole civilisations on.

The events recounted in the Bible also occurred during very credulous periods, where there were precious few other explanations to provide satisfactory and clear-cut answers to events at the time. The accounts of these events at the time would certainly not convince anyone in the business of news reporting today.

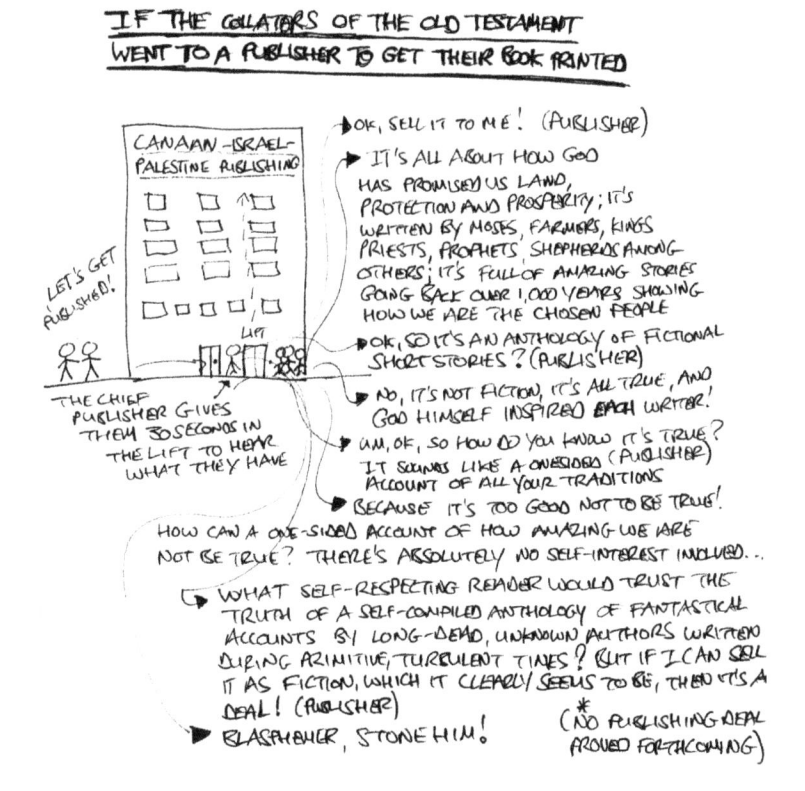

IF THE COLLATORS OF THE OLD TESTAMENT WENT TO A PUBLISHER TO GET THEIR BOOK PRINTED

- OK, SELL IT TO ME! (PUBLISHER)
- IT'S ALL ABOUT HOW GOD HAS PROMISED US LAND, PROTECTION AND PROSPERITY; IT'S WRITTEN BY MOSES, FARMERS, KINGS, PRIESTS, PROPHETS, SHEPHERDS AMONG OTHERS; IT'S FULL OF AMAZING STORIES GOING BACK OVER 1,000 YEARS SHOWING HOW WE ARE THE CHOSEN PEOPLE
- OK, SO IT'S AN ANTHOLOGY OF FICTIONAL SHORT STORIES? (PUBLISHER)
- NO, IT'S NOT FICTION, IT'S ALL TRUE, AND GOD HIMSELF INSPIRED EACH WRITER!
- UM, OK, SO HOW DO YOU KNOW IT'S TRUE? IT SOUNDS LIKE A ONE-SIDED (PUBLISHER) ACCOUNT OF ALL YOUR TRADITIONS
- BECAUSE IT'S TOO GOOD NOT TO BE TRUE! HOW CAN A ONE-SIDED ACCOUNT OF HOW AMAZING WE ARE NOT BE TRUE? THERE'S ABSOLUTELY NO SELF-INTEREST INVOLVED...
  - WHAT SELF-RESPECTING READER WOULD TRUST THE TRUTH OF A SELF-COMPILED ANTHOLOGY OF FANTASTICAL ACCOUNTS BY LONG-DEAD, UNKNOWN AUTHORS WRITTEN DURING PRIMITIVE, TURBULENT TIMES? BUT IF I CAN SELL IT AS FICTION, WHICH IT CLEARLY SEEMS TO BE, THEN IT'S A DEAL! (PUBLISHER)
- BLASPHEMER, STONE HIM!

(* NO PUBLISHING DEAL PROVED FORTHCOMING)

CANAAN-ISRAEL-PALESTINE PUBLISHING

LET'S GET PUBLISHED!

THE CHIEF PUBLISHER GIVES THEM 30 SECONDS IN THE LIFT TO HEAR WHAT THEY HAVE

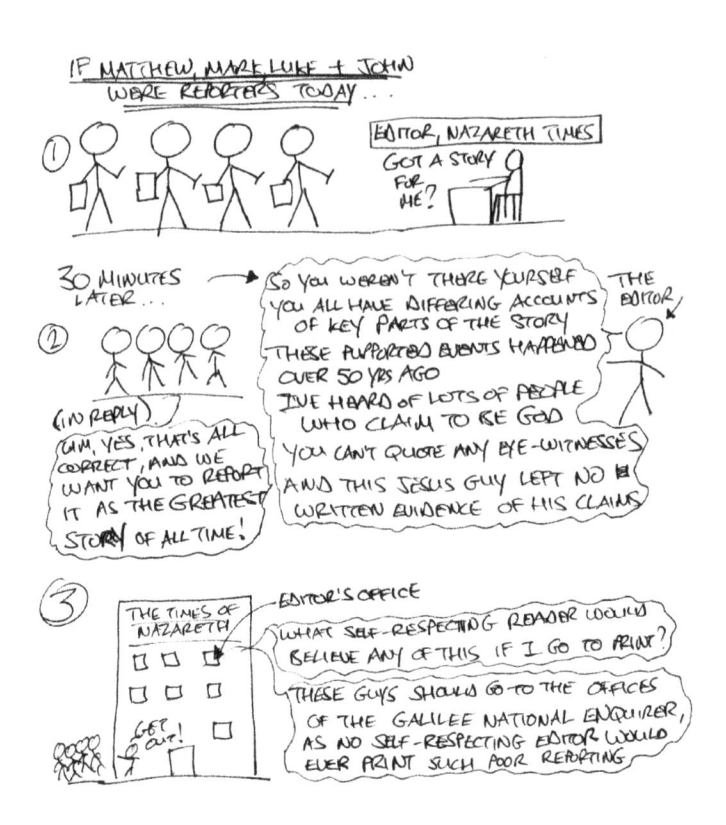

[Cartoon: "IF MATTHEW, MARK, LUKE + JOHN WERE REPORTERS TODAY..."

Panel 1: Four stick figures approach an editor — "EDITOR, NAZARETH TIMES GOT A STORY FOR ME?"

Panel 2: "30 MINUTES LATER..." The editor responds: "SO YOU WEREN'T THERE YOURSELF, YOU ALL HAVE DIFFERING ACCOUNTS OF KEY PARTS OF THE STORY, THESE PURPORTED EVENTS HAPPENED OVER 50 YRS AGO, I'VE HEARD OF LOTS OF PEOPLE WHO CLAIM TO BE GOD, YOU CAN'T QUOTE ANY EYE-WITNESSES, AND THIS JESUS GUY LEFT NO WRITTEN EVIDENCE OF HIS CLAIMS". (IN REPLY): "UM, YES, THAT'S ALL CORRECT, AND WE WANT YOU TO REPORT IT AS THE GREATEST STORY OF ALL TIME!"

Panel 3: THE TIMES OF NAZARETH building — EDITOR'S OFFICE: "WHAT SELF-RESPECTING READER WOULD BELIEVE ANY OF THIS IF I GO TO PRINT? THESE GUYS SHOULD GO TO THE OFFICES OF THE GALILEE NATIONAL ENQUIRER, AS NO SELF-RESPECTING EDITOR WOULD EVER PRINT SUCH POOR REPORTING". "GET OUT!"]

Surely God would have known that his approach of revealing himself through dreams and visions to a few individuals would create more questions than answers?

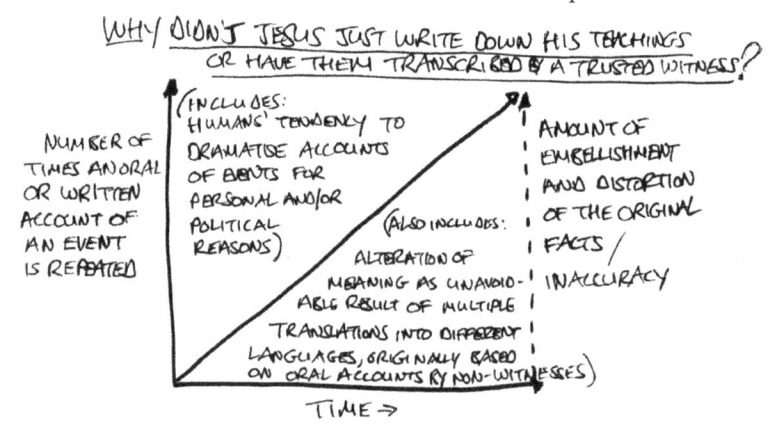

[Graph: "WHY DIDN'T JESUS JUST WRITE DOWN HIS TEACHINGS OR HAVE THEM TRANSCRIBED BY A TRUSTED WITNESS?"

Y-axis: NUMBER OF TIMES AN ORAL OR WRITTEN ACCOUNT OF AN EVENT IS REPEATED. X-axis: TIME →. Diagonal line going up, with labels: (INCLUDES: HUMANS' TENDENCY TO DRAMATISE ACCOUNTS OF EVENTS FOR PERSONAL AND/OR POLITICAL REASONS) (ALSO INCLUDES: ALTERATION OF MEANING AS UNAVOIDABLE RESULT OF MULTIPLE TRANSLATIONS INTO DIFFERENT LANGUAGES, ORIGINALLY BASED ON ORAL ACCOUNTS BY NON-WITNESSES). Right side: AMOUNT OF EMBELLISHMENT AND DISTORTION OF THE ORIGINAL FACTS / INACCURACY]

And when the accounts were written down, it seems that God inspired the Bible's authors to include a lot of contradictions and prophesies that subsequently proved untrue.

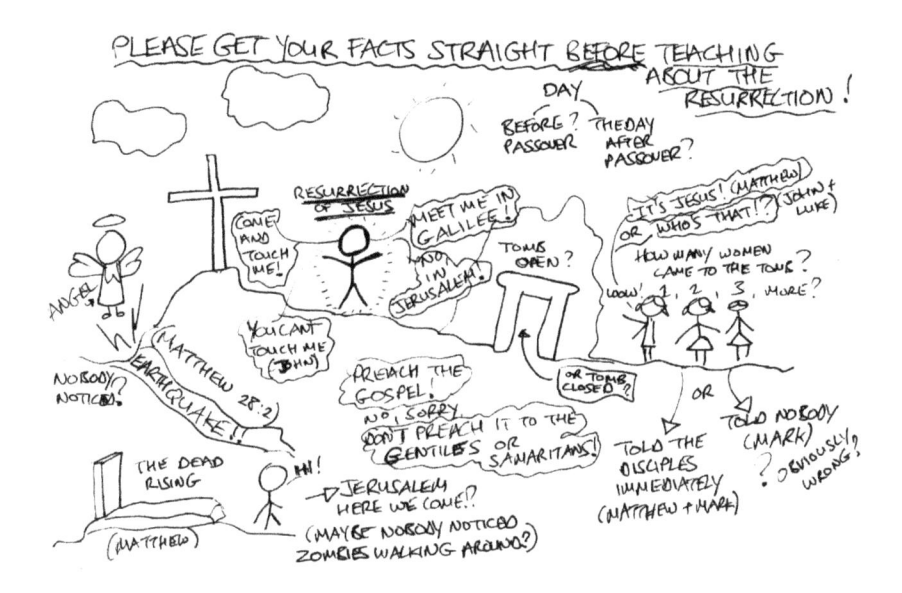

[Hand-drawn cartoon titled "PLEASE GET YOUR FACTS STRAIGHT BEFORE TEACHING ABOUT THE RESURRECTION!" showing multiple contradictions between Gospel accounts: Day before Passover? The day after Passover?; Resurrection of Jesus; Come and touch me! / You can't touch me (John); Meet me in Galilee / No, in Jerusalem; Tomb open? or Tomb closed?; It's Jesus! (Matthew) or Who's that? (John & Luke); How many women came to the tomb? 1, 2, 3, more?; Nobody noticed / Matthew 28:2 earthquake; The dead rising (Matthew) — maybe nobody noticed zombies walking around?; Preach the gospel / No, sorry, don't preach it to the Gentiles or Samaritans; Jerusalem here we come!; Told the disciples immediately (Matthew + Mark) or Told nobody (Mark) — obviously wrong.]

Even prophesies of Jesus himself did not come to pass.

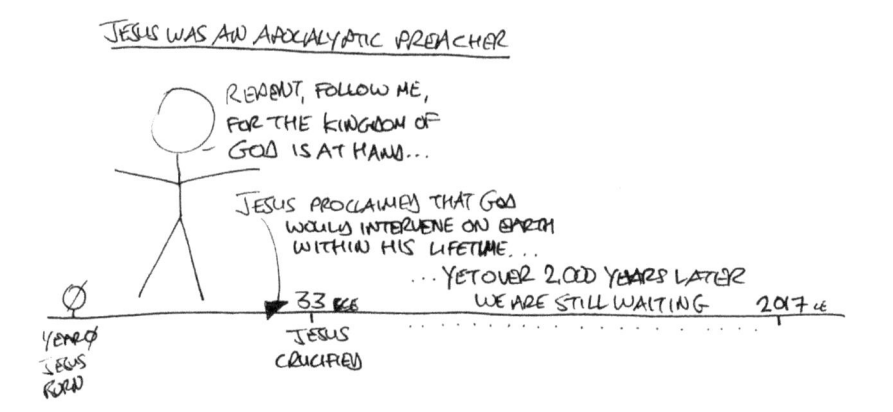

[Hand-drawn timeline titled "JESUS WAS AN APOCALYPTIC PREACHER" with stick figure saying "Repent, follow me, for the kingdom of God is at hand..." Jesus proclaimed that God would intervene on earth within his lifetime... Yet over 2,000 years later we are still waiting. Timeline: Year 0 Jesus born — 33 CE Jesus crucified — 2017 CE]

103

Why is the ultimate reward, eternal life in God's presence, so vaguely defined?

[Hand-drawn diagram of heaven's gates surrounded by questions: BOREDOM? ACTIVITIES? GOLF? ETERNAL LIFE? (INFINITE?) HUMAN BODIES? NEED FOR FOOD & WATER? ETERNAL MARRIAGE? SEX? GOVERNANCE? SOLID MATTER? DAY/NIGHT/SLEEP? LOTS OF PRAYING AND WORSHIP ✓ WORK? PETS? SEX? MEMORIES? LOCATION? JUDGEMENT DAY / REVELATIONS / RESURRECTION OF THE DEAD? THOSE WHO DIED BEFORE JESUS WAS BORN?

IF HEAVEN IS THE ULTIMATE REWARD AND GOAL OF RELIGIOUS BELIEVERS, WHY IS IT SO POORLY DEFINED?]

Religion has been passed down by thousands of different people over thousands of years. This evokes in me an image of the game Chinese whispers.

[Hand-drawn diagram titled "DIVINE REVELATION AND CHINESE WHISPERS" showing flow from TRUTH → TRANSMISSION → INTERMEDIARY (e.g. Angel Gabriel) → PROPHET → NORMAL PEOPLE → SUBSEQUENT GENERATIONS, with annotations: SOURCE CREDIBLE / CORRUPTED / SUPERCEDED? COULD MESSAGE BE INTERCEPTED AND CHANGED MALICIOUSLY? DISTANCE TRAVELLED? POSSIBILITIES FOR DISTORTION? TIME LAG? (ANOTHER REVELATION ON ITS WAY?) INTERPRETED AND RELAYED WITHOUT DISTORTION? ULTERIOR MOTIVES? INFILTRATED BY THE DEVIL? ANALOG vs DIGITAL! DESIRE FOR COMFORTING NEWS, AND TO BE SPECIAL RECIPIENTS! HOW CREDULOUS? REVERENCE FOR PERCEIVED AUTHORITY? CULTURAL AND HISTORICAL CONTEXT CAN FRAME MESSAGES DIFFERENTLY; EMPHASIS CHANGED FOR POLITICAL OR PERSONAL GAIN? CONFIRMATION BIAS? LESS THAN PERFECT MENTAL AND PSYCHOLOGICAL STATE? FALLIBILITY OF ORAL TRANSMISSION OVER MULTIPLE GENERATIONS? TRANSLATION OF SUBTLE TERMS THROUGH DIFFERENT LANGUAGES? CHOICE OF MESSAGES DECIDED BY COMMITTEE FOR UNKNOWN REASONS? 100% CONVICTION THAT THE 'TRUTH' OF DIVINE REVELATION PERFECTLY PRESERVED? A SUFFICIENT BASIS FOR MORAL FOUNDATION OF SOCIETY?]

Belief in the claims of religion therefore requires huge leaps of credulity.

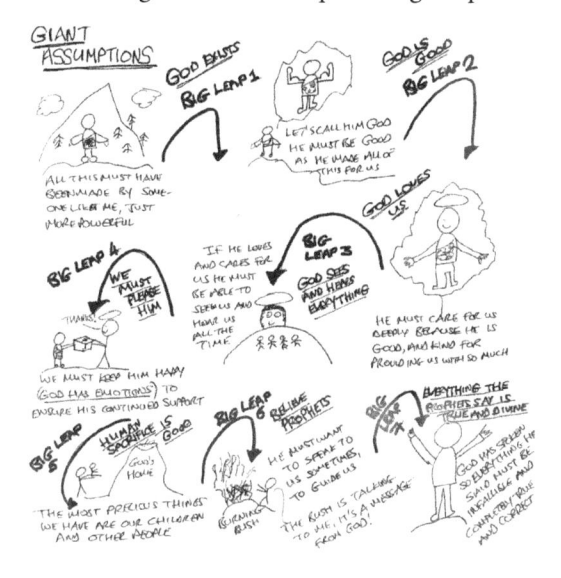

I had a dream a few years ago that I was with the late Christopher Hitchens on a moped driving along a road in a nice town by a lake somewhere warm. I realise this was just a dream and nothing more, but should this be regarded as a supernatural event?

We shouldn't allow our lives, societies and cultures to be dominated by extraordinary claims that lack any of the necessary extraordinary evidence.

It also seems hypocritical for adherents of Judaism, Christianity or Islam to attack each other's claims as false when they share so many characteristics and foundation accounts.

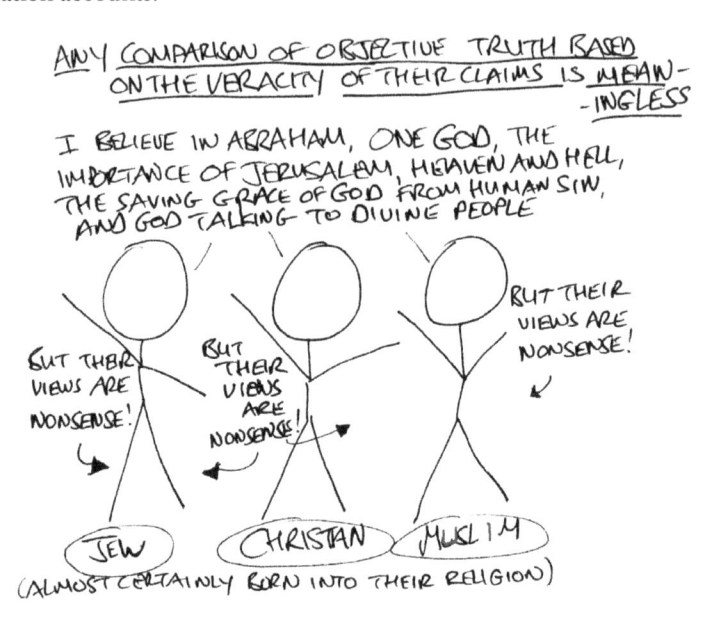

ANY COMPARISON OF OBJECTIVE TRUTH BASED ON THE VERACITY OF THEIR CLAIMS IS MEANINGLESS

I BELIEVE IN ABRAHAM, ONE GOD, THE IMPORTANCE OF JERUSALEM, HEAVEN AND HELL, THE SAVING GRACE OF GOD FROM HUMAN SIN, AND GOD TALKING TO DIVINE PEOPLE

BUT THEIR VIEWS ARE NONSENSE! — JEW
BUT THEIR VIEWS ARE NONSENSE! — CHRISTIAN
BUT THEIR VIEWS ARE NONSENSE! — MUSLIM

(ALMOST CERTAINLY BORN INTO THEIR RELIGION)

One wouldn't take at face value the claims of one salesperson about a second-hand car (and the comparison with religion isn't so far-fetched; religion is after all the retelling of stories down the ages, like stories about a car told by different owners).

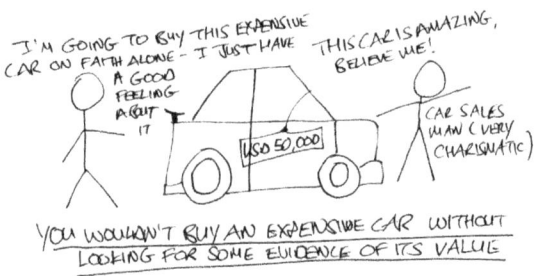

I'M GOING TO BUY THIS EXPENSIVE CAR ON FAITH ALONE — I JUST HAVE A GOOD FEELING ABOUT IT

THIS CAR IS AMAZING, BELIEVE ME! — CAR SALESMAN (VERY CHARISMATIC)

USD 50,000

YOU WOULDN'T BUY AN EXPENSIVE CAR WITHOUT LOOKING FOR SOME EVIDENCE OF ITS VALUE

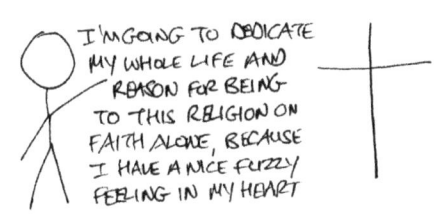

> I'M GOING TO DEDICATE MY WHOLE LIFE AND REASON FOR BEING TO THIS RELIGION ON FAITH ALONE, BECAUSE I HAVE A NICE FUZZY FEELING IN MY HEART
>
> SO WHY WOULD YOU COMMIT YOUR WHOLE LIFE TO A BELIEF SYSTEM WITHOUT AT LEAST ASKING YOURSELF IF IT'S REALLY WORTHY OF YOUR SUBMISSION?

13. Biblical Christianity is not Catholicism

I also didn't realise what a large gulf exists between the teachings of Jesus and the religious doctrines pronounced by the Roman Catholic Church.

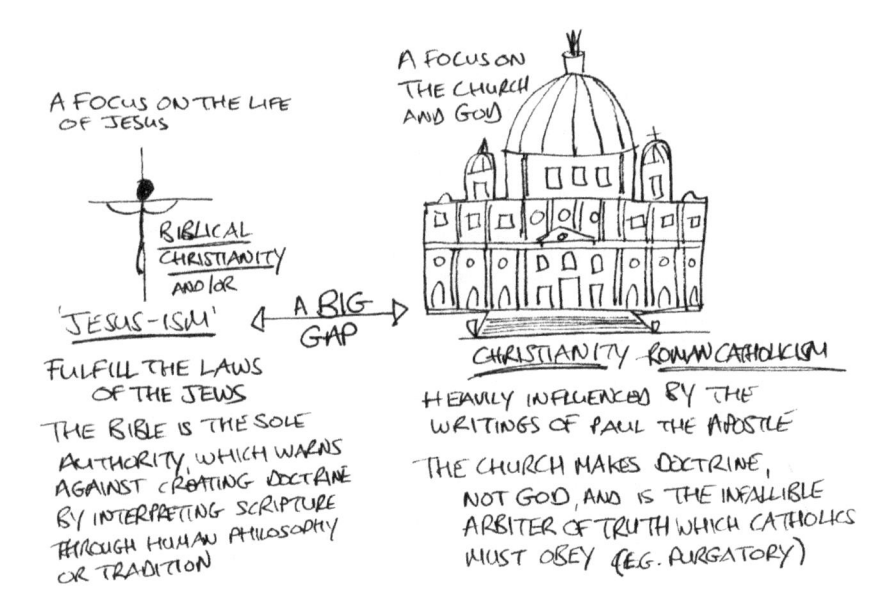

A FOCUS ON THE LIFE OF JESUS

BIBLICAL CHRISTIANITY AND/OR 'JESUS-ISM'

⬅ A BIG GAP ➡

FULFILL THE LAWS OF THE JEWS

THE BIBLE IS THE SOLE AUTHORITY, WHICH WARNS AGAINST CREATING DOCTRINE BY INTERPRETING SCRIPTURE THROUGH HUMAN PHILOSOPHY OR TRADITION

A FOCUS ON THE CHURCH AND GOD

CHRISTIANITY - ROMAN CATHOLICISM

HEAVILY INFLUENCED BY THE WRITINGS OF PAUL THE APOSTLE

THE CHURCH MAKES DOCTRINE, NOT GOD, AND IS THE INFALLIBLE ARBITER OF TRUTH WHICH CATHOLICS MUST OBEY (EG. PURGATORY)

One could even argue that Jesus was not a Christian, which would negate any of the authority claimed by the Church.

JESUS WAS NOT A CHRISTIAN?

[Sketch: stick figure labeled with "Jewish Parents", "Raised in Judaism", "Nazareth", "Jewish Teacher", "Jewish Followers"]

"I HAVE COME TO FULFILL THE LAW AND THE PROPHETS. YOU WON'T ENTER HEAVEN UNLESS YOUR RIGHTEOUSNESS SURPASSES THAT OF THE PHARISEES..."

What gives the Church authority to set doctrine when they are clearly fallible men? Look at the Church's attempts to cover up its child rape scandals. And just because a recent pope proclaimed papal infallibility doesn't make it so.

A key text of the Catholic Church, the Nicene Creed, was defined by a group of fourth-century men meeting in Nicaea under the leadership of a Roman emperor.

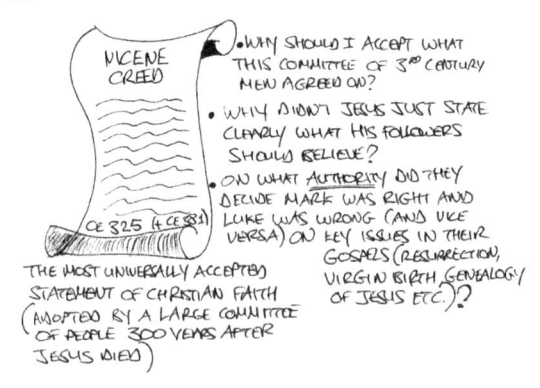

[Sketch: scroll labeled "NICENE CREED, CE 325 (4CE??)"]

THE MOST UNIVERSALLY ACCEPTED STATEMENT OF CHRISTIAN FAITH (ADOPTED BY A LARGE COMMITTEE OF PEOPLE 300 YEARS AFTER JESUS DIED)

- WHY SHOULD I ACCEPT WHAT THIS COMMITTEE OF 3RD CENTURY MEN AGREED ON?
- WHY DIDN'T JESUS JUST STATE CLEARLY WHAT HIS FOLLOWERS SHOULD BELIEVE?
- ON WHAT AUTHORITY DID THEY DECIDE MARK WAS RIGHT AND LUKE WAS WRONG (AND VICE VERSA) ON KEY ISSUES IN THEIR GOSPELS (RESURRECTION, VIRGIN BIRTH, GENEALOGY OF JESUS ETC.)?

How can this be regarded as anything more than just the best guess of many possibly well-intentioned men about the teachings of a preacher who died hundreds of years earlier, when all they had to go on were differing accounts written by people who weren't with Jesus at the time? How can they extrapolate this creed from hotly contended, differing interpretations of the teachings, and indeed, nature of this man? How can they claim it is 100% true and now cast in stone? We also know that any text ratified by committee is going to include compromises and fudges, furthering weakening its claims to authenticity.

14. Religion in context – a possibly infinite universe

The three Abrahamic religions evolved in a time of relative ignorance, so it is understandable that their cosmic framework was very limited, focusing on the earth as the centre of the universe and the apple of God's eye.

But in 1925 this framework was well and truly shattered for good, when astronomer Edwin Hubble showed that we are just one planet within a vast expanse of other galaxies. This realisation should surely call into doubt continued religious claims that we are the special children of God, who sees us and cares for us? Suddenly, we shrank from being the centre of the universe to being one drop in a possibly infinite ocean, unimaginably deep and wide. How then to see religious claims in this new vast context?

THE DAY RELIGION DIED?
(THE FIRST PROOF GOD MADE THE WORLD IN A TINY BACK ALLEY IN NOWHERESVILLE)

WOW SO MANY OTHER GALAXIES! WE ARE SO TINY!

EDWIN HUBBLE 1925

RELIGIOUS CLAIMS THAT THE WORLD IS AT THE CENTRE OF COSMIC AFFAIRS, RECEDING INTO THE DISTANCE, AWAY FROM CREDIBILITY AND REASON

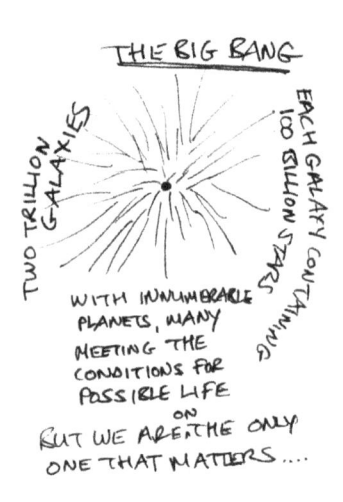

[Hand-drawn diagram: THE BIG BANG — with rays emanating from a central point, labeled "TWO TRILLION GALAXIES" and "EACH GALAXY CONTAINING 100 BILLION STARS", with text below: "WITH INNUMERABLE PLANETS, MANY MEETING THE CONDITIONS FOR POSSIBLE LIFE BUT WE ARE THE ONLY ONE ON THAT MATTERS...."]

All the evidence overwhelmingly points to the universe starting with the Big Bang, with the subsequent creation of perhaps two trillion galaxies, each containing hundreds of millions of stars and planets (if not more). Against this background it seems awfully conceited to regard ourselves as the most important object out of almost countless others.

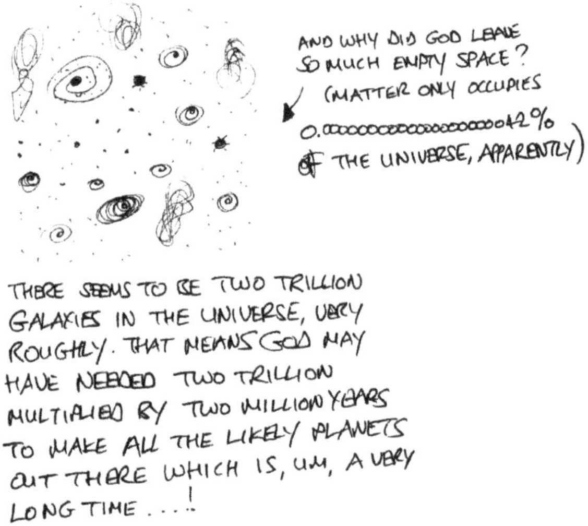

[Hand-drawn sketch of galaxies and stars with caption: "AND WHY DID GOD LEAVE SO MUCH EMPTY SPACE? (MATTER ONLY OCCUPIES 0.0000000000000000042% OF THE UNIVERSE, APPARENTLY)"]

[Caption below: "THERE SEEMS TO BE TWO TRILLION GALAXIES IN THE UNIVERSE, VERY ROUGHLY. THAT MEANS GOD MAY HAVE NEEDED TWO TRILLION MULTIPLIED BY TWO MILLION YEARS TO MAKE ALL THE LIKELY PLANETS OUT THERE WHICH IS, UM, A VERY LONG TIME....!"]

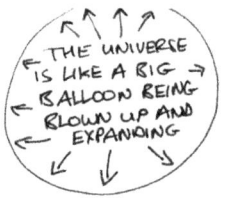

(handwritten in circle with arrows) THE UNIVERSE IS LIKE A BIG BALLOON BEING BLOWN UP AND EXPANDING

(handwritten) GALAXIES ARE EXPANDING AWAY FROM EACH OTHER AT 150,000 M.P.H. WHILE SOME, VERY FAR AWAY, ARE FLYING AWAY FROM US FASTER THAN THE SPEED OF LIGHT (APPARENTLY!)

God must have needed millions, if not billions of years, to make all those planets out there.

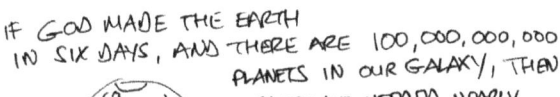

(handwritten) IF GOD MADE THE EARTH IN SIX DAYS, AND THERE ARE 100,000,000,000 PLANETS IN OUR GALAXY, THEN PERHAPS HE NEEDED NEARLY TWO MILLION YEARS (INCLUDING REST DAYS) TO MAKE THEM ALL? (THAT'S LEAVING OUT THE 400 BILLION STARS AND THE POSSIBLE 400 MILLION BLACK HOLES IN THE MILKY WAY)

Maybe this is what he was doing for all those billions of years before the earth formed.

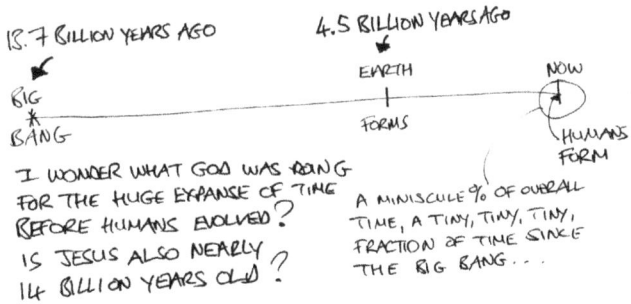

(handwritten timeline) 13.7 BILLION YEARS AGO — BIG BANG ... 4.5 BILLION YEARS AGO — EARTH FORMS ... NOW — HUMANS FORM

I WONDER WHAT GOD WAS DOING FOR THE HUGE EXPANSE OF TIME BEFORE HUMANS EVOLVED? IS JESUS ALSO NEARLY 14 BILLION YEARS OLD?

A MINISCULE % OF OVERALL TIME, A TINY, TINY, TINY, FRACTION OF TIME SINCE THE BIG BANG...

He must also have the most amazing GPS-type tracker system.

HOW CAN GOD KEEP TRACK OF WHERE WE ARE IN THE UNIVERSE?

THE SUN

THE EARTH IS TRAVELING THROUGH SPACE AROUND THE SUN AT 67,000 M.P.H.

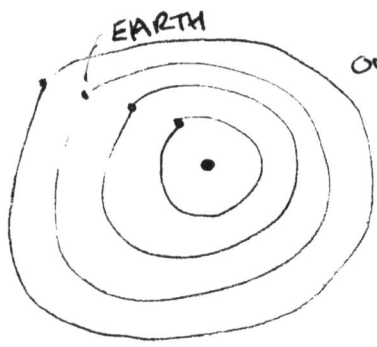

OUR SOLAR SYSTEM IS FLYING AROUND THE CENTRE OF OUR GALAXY AT 490,000 M.P.H.

EARTH

OUR GALAXY IS SPEEDING THROUGH THE UNIVERSE AT 1.3 MILLION M.P.H

And time itself is relative in these conditions, depending on the mass of an object and its speed of travel.

JESUS WILL NEED VERY SPECIFIC SPACETIME CO-ORDINATES IF/WHEN HE IS TO COME AGAIN TO EARTH

OBSERVABLE THE UNIVERSE

UNIVERSE EXPANSION AT SPEED OF LIGHT

GALAXIES FLYING AROUND AT A MILLION M.P.H.

SOLAR SYSTEMS RAPIDLY MOVING WITHIN GALAXIES
PLANETS WHIZZING AROUND STARS WITHIN SOLAR SYSTEMS

DIAMETER OF THE UNIVERSE IS 93 BILLION LIGHT YEARS*

*AND LIGHT CAN GO AROUND THE EARTH 7.5 TIMES IN ONE SECOND

AND I WILL ALSO HAVE TO AVOID THE BILLIONS OF BLACK HOLES DOTTED AROUND THE UNIVERSE

JESUS

IF/WHEN EXTRA-TERRESTRIAL LIFE IS FOUND, WILL WE FEEL THAT GOD HAS DECEIVED US AS WE ARE NOT HIS ONLY CHILDREN? IT MIGHT FEEL LIKE OUR STEP-FATHER HAS BEEN HIDING HIS SECOND FAMILY FROM US...

ALIEN LIFE ON EXO PLANET

What if God has to save all these likely beings as well?

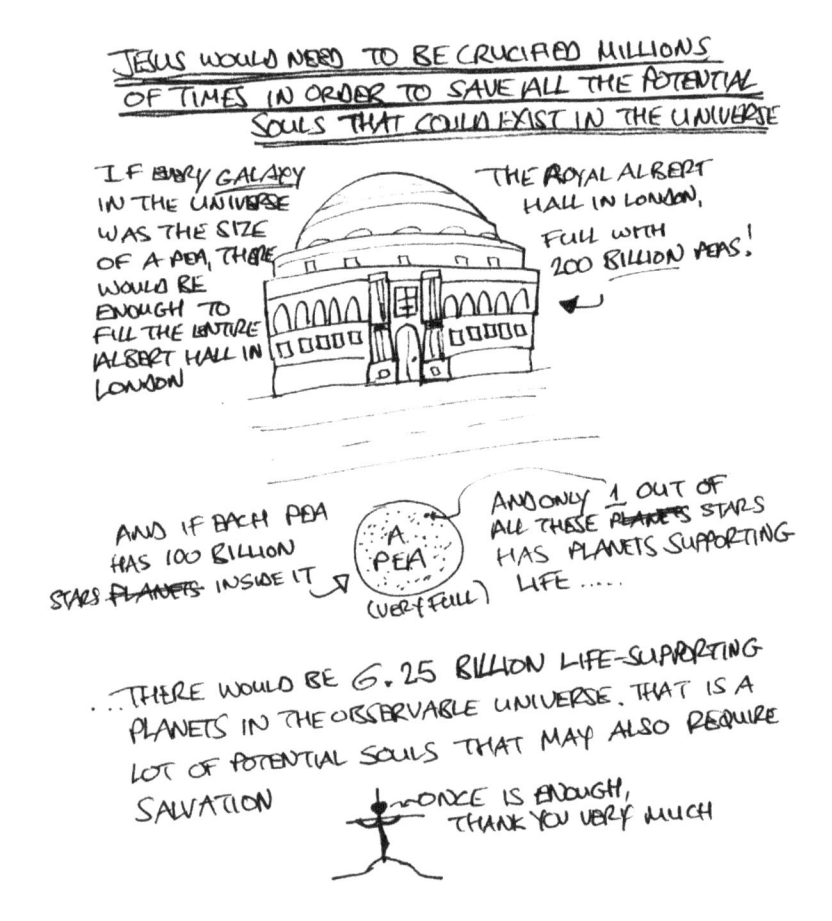

JESUS WOULD NEED TO BE CRUCIFIED MILLIONS OF TIMES IN ORDER TO SAVE ALL THE POTENTIAL SOULS THAT COULD EXIST IN THE UNIVERSE

IF EVERY GALAXY IN THE UNIVERSE WAS THE SIZE OF A PEA, THERE WOULD BE ENOUGH TO FILL THE ENTIRE ALBERT HALL IN LONDON

THE ROYAL ALBERT HALL IN LONDON, FULL WITH 200 BILLION PEAS!

AND IF EACH PEA HAS 100 BILLION STARS ~~PLANETS~~ INSIDE IT

A PEA (VERY FULL)

AND ONLY 1 OUT OF ALL THESE ~~PLANETS~~ STARS HAS PLANETS SUPPORTING LIFE......

...THERE WOULD BE 6.25 BILLION LIFE-SUPPORTING PLANETS IN THE OBSERVABLE UNIVERSE. THAT IS A LOT OF POTENTIAL SOULS THAT MAY ALSO REQUIRE SALVATION

ONCE IS ENOUGH, THANK YOU VERY MUCH

I've often wondered how prayers work, if/when God is residing in heaven.

HOW DO PRAYERS WORK?

SOUND WAVES ONLY TRAVEL A CERTAIN DISTANCE (PRAYER)

THE MODERN WORLD HAS LOTS OF NOISE POLLUTION — BEEP BEEP!, CHAT CHAT, ROAD REPAIRS

SOUND CAN'T TRAVEL THROUGH A VACUUM — 🌍 → VACUUM → HEAVEN

PRAYERS ARE OFTEN WHISPERED SO ARE EVEN MORE DIFFICULT TO RECEIVE (WHISPER....)

AND DOESN'T GOD KNOW WHAT WE WANT ANYWAY?

To cover the vast distances between the abode of God, and us, they must travel faster than the speed of light (theoretically not possible however).

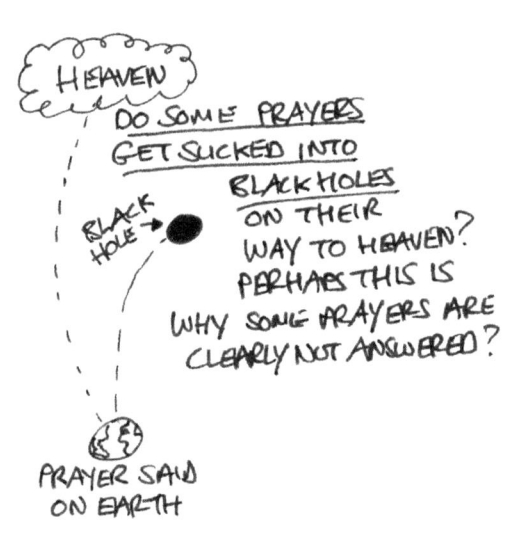

HEAVEN

DO SOME PRAYERS GET SUCKED INTO BLACK HOLES ON THEIR WAY TO HEAVEN? PERHAPS THIS IS WHY SOME PRAYERS ARE CLEARLY NOT ANSWERED?

BLACK HOLE →

PRAYER SAID ON EARTH

And how do we travel to heaven after we die?

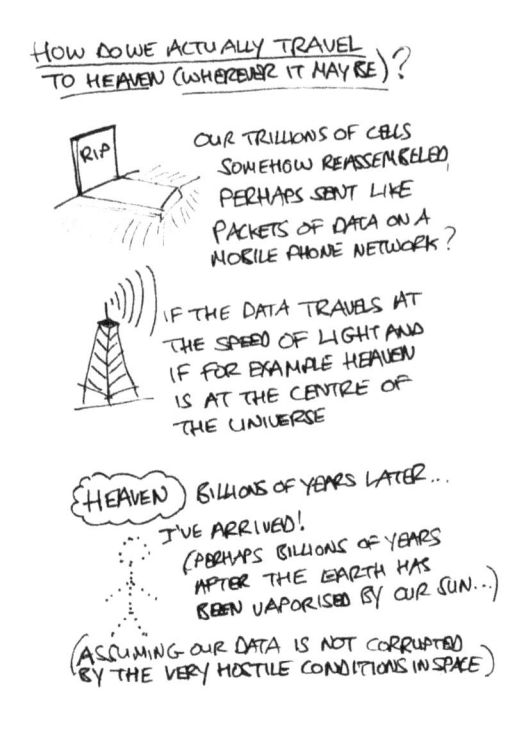

How do we actually travel to heaven (wherever it may be)?

RIP — Our trillions of cells somehow reassembled, perhaps sent like packets of data on a mobile phone network?

If the data travels at the speed of light and if for example heaven is at the centre of the universe

HEAVEN — Billions of years later... I've arrived! (Perhaps billions of years after the Earth has been vaporised by our sun...)

(Assuming our data is not corrupted by the very hostile conditions in space)

The God of the Old Testament implied there were other Gods. Perhaps these exist elsewhere in the vast expanse of space?

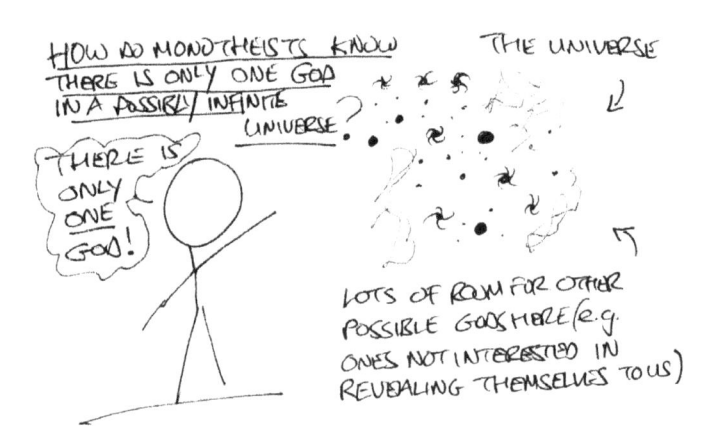

How do monotheists know there is only one God in a possibly infinite universe?

THE UNIVERSE

"There is only one God!"

Lots of room for other possible Gods here (e.g. ones not interested in revealing themselves to us)

Science is revealing more and more to us each day, about the workings of the universe.

> QUANTUM MECHANICS
> +
> GRAVITY
> CAN = POP!
> BANG!
> UNIVERSES POPPING INTO EXISTENCE
>
> SO NO NEED FOR A CREATOR (GOD) *
> (* ANYWAY, WHO/WHAT CREATED GOD?)

A bit of a silly, but perhaps illustrative point here, that humans were in no way the only interest of God when he allegedly created our planet.

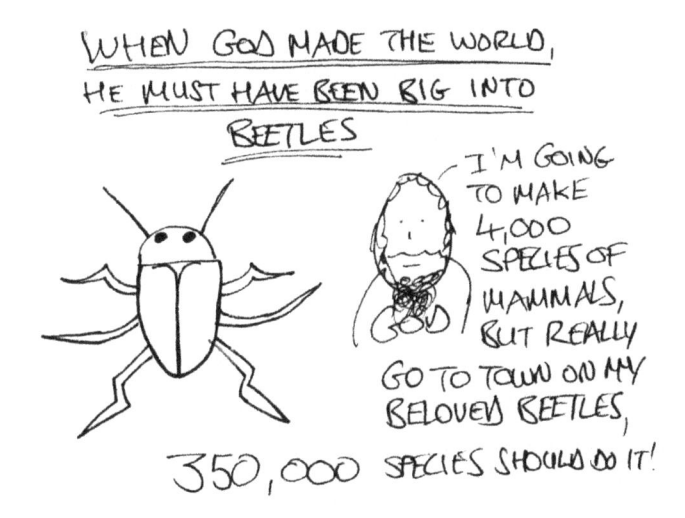

> WHEN GOD MADE THE WORLD, HE MUST HAVE BEEN BIG INTO BEETLES
>
> I'M GOING TO MAKE 4,000 SPECIES OF MAMMALS, BUT REALLY GO TO TOWN ON MY BELOVED BEETLES, 350,000 SPECIES SHOULD DO IT!

It's hard to ignore the fact that religion has been a hindrance to scientific discovery over the last 500 years or so.

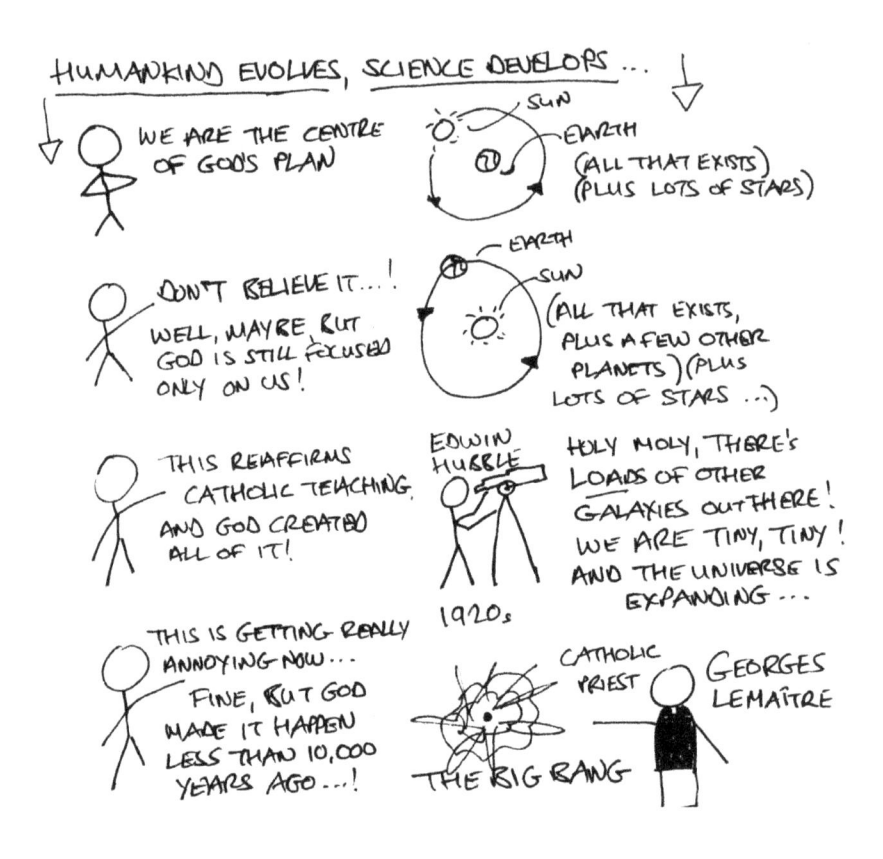

[Hand-drawn cartoon illustration titled "HUMANKIND EVOLVES, SCIENCE DEVELOPS..." depicting a dialogue between stick figures about the evolving understanding of the universe:

- *Figure: "WE ARE THE CENTRE OF GOD'S PLAN" — with diagram of Earth at centre, Sun orbiting (ALL THAT EXISTS) (PLUS LOTS OF STARS)*
- *Figure: "DON'T BELIEVE IT...!" / "WELL, MAYBE BUT GOD IS STILL FOCUSED ONLY ON US!" — with diagram of Sun at centre, Earth orbiting (ALL THAT EXISTS, PLUS A FEW OTHER PLANETS) (PLUS LOTS OF STARS...)*
- *Figure: "THIS REAFFIRMS CATHOLIC TEACHING. AND GOD CREATED ALL OF IT!" — Edwin Hubble (1920s) with telescope: "HOLY MOLY, THERE'S LOADS OF OTHER GALAXIES OUT THERE! WE ARE TINY, TINY! AND THE UNIVERSE IS EXPANDING..."*
- *Figure: "THIS IS GETTING REALLY ANNOYING NOW... FINE, BUT GOD MADE IT HAPPEN LESS THAN 10,000 YEARS AGO...!" — Catholic priest Georges Lemaître with "THE BIG BANG"]*

15. Why do we need God?

In the context of evolution, it seems clear now that morality predates religion, otherwise we would not have evolved successfully as primates. There is significant evidence now to show that we share moral traits like empathy and cooperation with other primates and other animals.

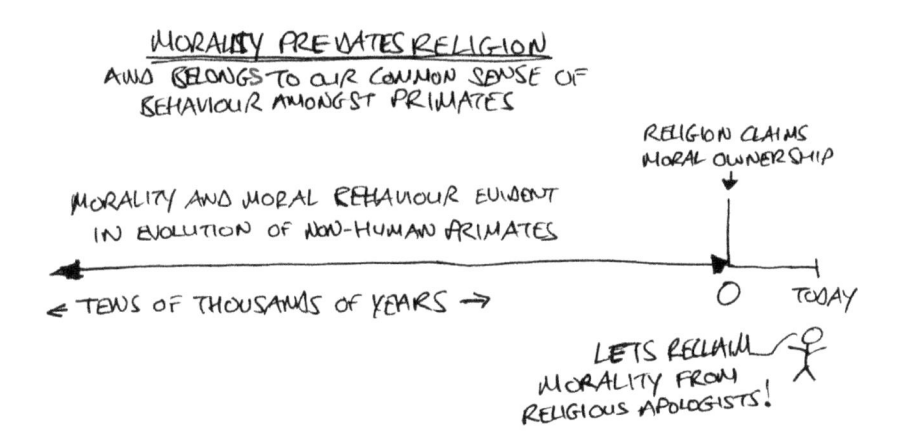

MORALITY PREDATES RELIGION
AND BELONGS TO OUR COMMON SENSE OF
BEHAVIOUR AMONGST PRIMATES

MORALITY AND MORAL BEHAVIOUR EVIDENT
IN EVOLUTION OF NON-HUMAN PRIMATES

RELIGION CLAIMS
MORAL OWNERSHIP

← TENS OF THOUSANDS OF YEARS →   0   TODAY

LETS RECLAIM
MORALITY FROM
RELIGIOUS APOLOGISTS!

The Bible, with its gruesome stories in the Old Testament, is certainly not a good moral guide.

WHY DO WE NEED GOD?

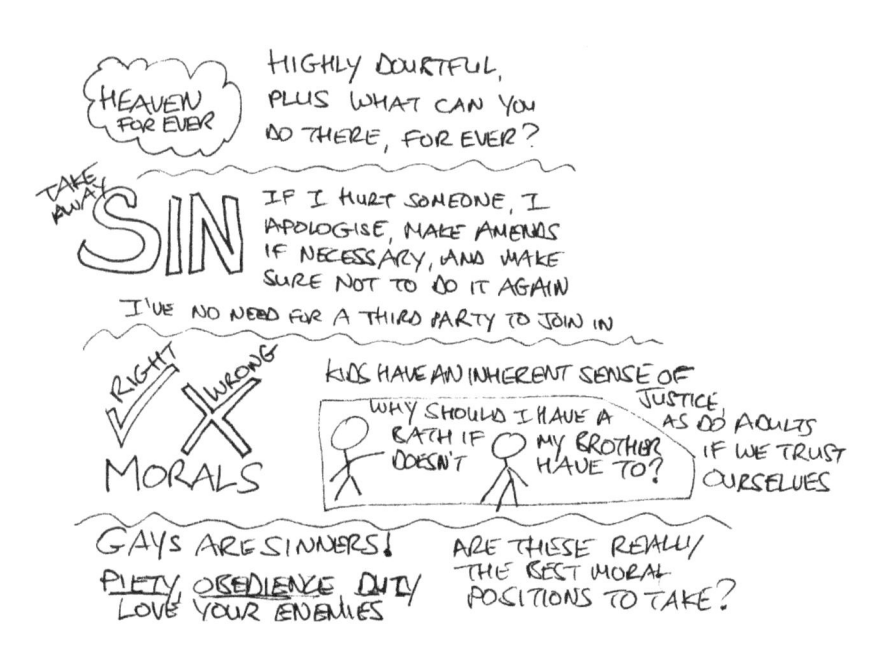

HEAVEN FOR EVER — HIGHLY DOUBTFUL, PLUS WHAT CAN YOU DO THERE, FOR EVER?

TAKE AWAY SIN — IF I HURT SOMEONE, I APOLOGISE, MAKE AMENDS IF NECESSARY, AND MAKE SURE NOT TO DO IT AGAIN
I'VE NO NEED FOR A THIRD PARTY TO JOIN IN

RIGHT ✓ WRONG ✗ MORALS

KIDS HAVE AN INHERENT SENSE OF JUSTICE,
"WHY SHOULD I HAVE A BATH IF MY BROTHER DOESN'T HAVE TO?"
AS DO ADULTS IF WE TRUST OURSELVES

GAYS ARE SINNERS!
PIETY, OBEDIENCE, DUTY
LOVE YOUR ENEMIES

ARE THESE REALLY THE BEST MORAL POSITIONS TO TAKE?

In addition, the teachings of Jesus are arguably not moral.

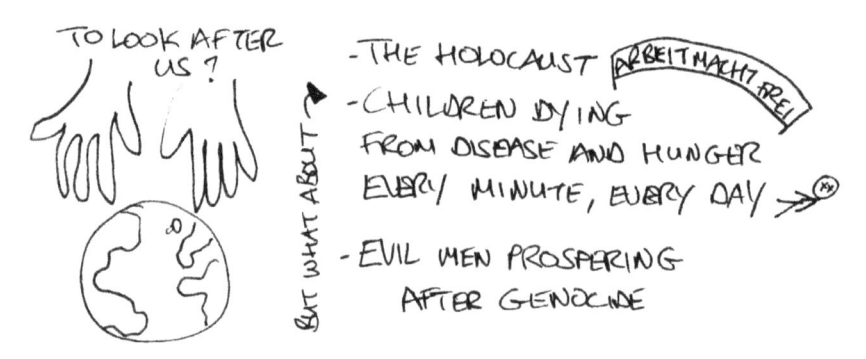

TO LOOK AFTER US?

BUT WHAT ABOUT

- THE HOLOCAUST ARBEIT MACHT FREI
- CHILDREN DYING FROM DISEASE AND HUNGER EVERY MINUTE, EVERY DAY
- EVIL MEN PROSPERING AFTER GENOCIDE

16. Many religious messages seem to me harmful for society

IMPLYING THAT PEOPLE ARE BEING PERMANENTLY JUDGED IS A DREADFUL INTRUSION OF PRIVACY

THREATENING PEOPLE WITH THE MOST EXTREME FORM OF NEVER-ENDING TORTURE IS DEPLORABLE AND EVIL

PROMOTING BELIEF IN SCIENTIFICALLY PROVED FALSEHOODS IS DISHONEST

TEACHING THAT PEOPLE ARE RESPONSIBLE FOR THE ACTS OF OTHERS, AND THAT THEY ARE INHERENTLY FLAWED BEINGS IS <u>ATROCIOUS</u> AND <u>SINISTER</u>

INDOCTRINATING CHILDREN BEFORE THEY CAN THINK FOR THEMSELVES IS <u>CRUEL AND ABUSIVE</u>

PROMOTING THE SUBMISSION OF ONESELF TO AN AUTHORITY IS <u>DEGRADING</u>

THE REGULAR SHAMING AND HUMILIATION OF BELIEVERS IS <u>BELITTLING</u> AND <u>DENIGRATING</u>

PLACING THE INTERESTS OF AN UNELECTED, UNACCOUNTABLE INSTITUTION THAT IS A LAW UNTO ITSELF ABOVE THOSE OF CHILDREN RAPED IN ITS CARE IS <u>HORRIFIC</u> AND <u>ABOMINABLE</u>

TEACHING THAT SEX IS IN ANY WAY WRONG IS <u>DEPLORABLE</u> AND <u>DAMAGING</u>

TEACHING THAT THE LOVE ONE FEELS FOR ANOTHER HUMAN BEING, REGARDLESS OF GENDER, IS <u>APPALLING</u>

IMPLYING THAT WOMEN ARE IN ANY WAY DEFICIENT TO MEN IS <u>SHAMEFUL</u>

17. Religion in charts

Some of my impressions of religion are best displayed in charts.

HOW BELIEVERS COME TO THEIR UNDOUBTING AND FULLY COMMITTED BELIEF IN THEIR ONE, TRUE RELIGION

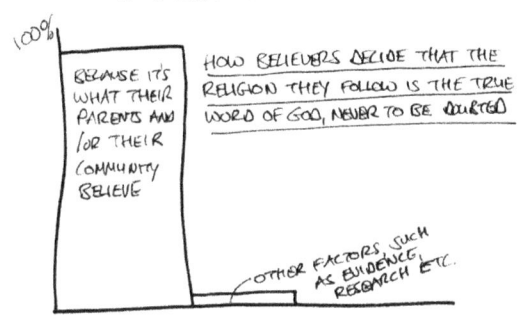

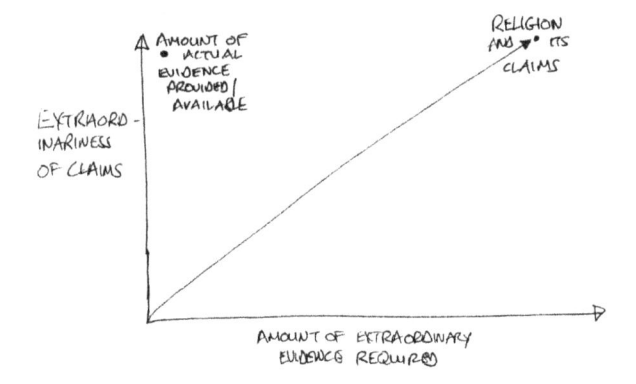

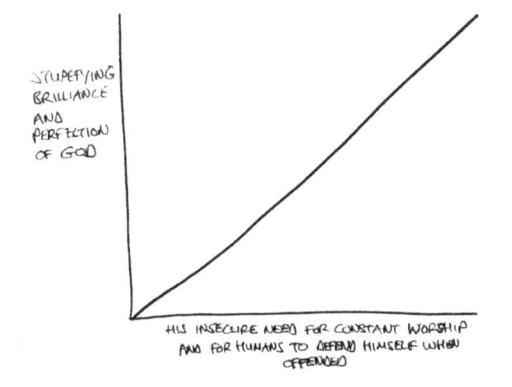

100%

BECAUSE IT'S WHAT THEIR PARENTS AND /OR THEIR COMMUNITY BELIEVE

HOW BELIEVERS DECIDE THAT THE RELIGION THEY FOLLOW IS THE TRUE WORD OF GOD, NEVER TO BE DOUBTED

OTHER FACTORS, SUCH AS EVIDENCE, RESEARCH ETC.

↑ AMOUNT OF ACTUAL EVIDENCE PROVIDED / AVAILABLE

EXTRAORDINARINESS OF CLAIMS

RELIGION AND ITS CLAIMS

AMOUNT OF EXTRAORDINARY EVIDENCE REQUIRED →

STUPEFYING BRILLIANCE AND PERFECTION OF GOD

HIS INSECURE NEED FOR CONSTANT WORSHIP AND FOR HUMANS TO DEFEND HIMSELF WHEN OFFENDED

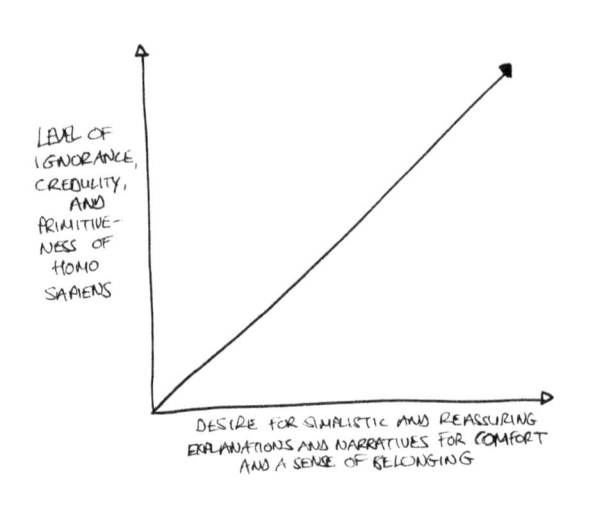

Graph 1:

Y-axis: LEVEL OF IGNORANCE, CREDULITY, AND PRIMITIVENESS OF HOMO SAPIENS

X-axis: DESIRE FOR SIMPLISTIC AND REASSURING EXPLANATIONS AND NARRATIVES FOR COMFORT AND A SENSE OF BELONGING

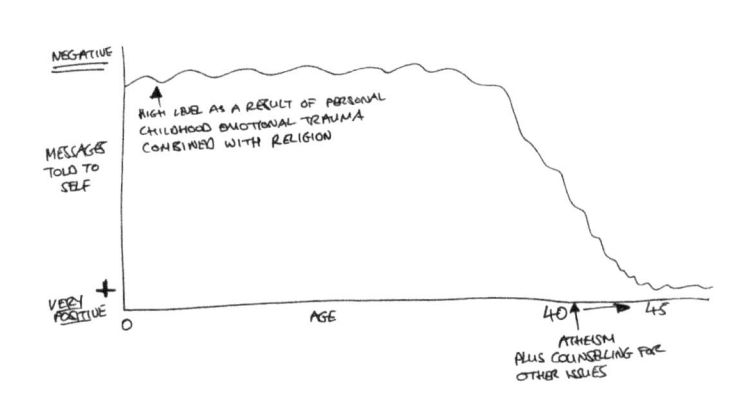

(Line rising diagonally from origin)

Graph 2:

Y-axis: MESSAGES TOLD TO SELF (from VERY POSITIVE at bottom to NEGATIVE at top)

X-axis: AGE (0 to 45)

Annotation at high level: HIGH LEVEL AS A RESULT OF PERSONAL CHILDHOOD EMOTIONAL TRAUMA COMBINED WITH RELIGION

Annotation at 40: ATHEISM PLUS COUNSELLING FOR OTHER ISSUES

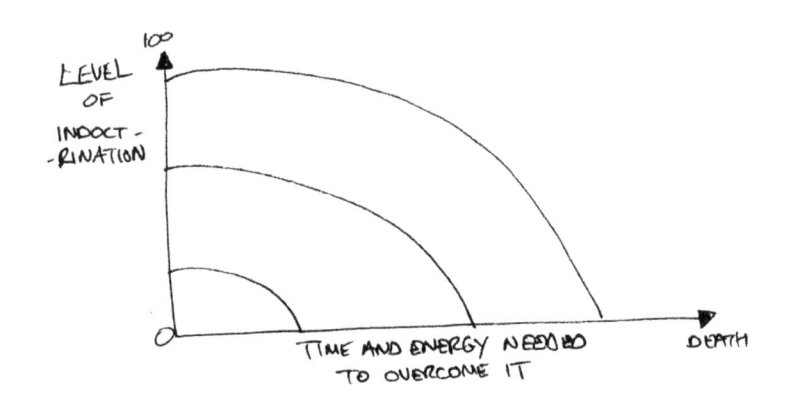

Graph 3:

Y-axis: LEVEL OF INDOCTRINATION (0 to 100)

X-axis: TIME AND ENERGY NEEDED TO OVERCOME IT → DEATH

(Three concentric quarter-circle arcs)

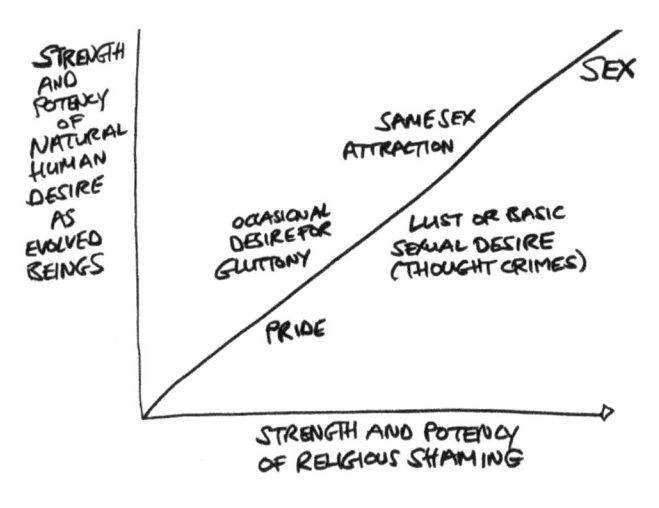

Chart 1 (axes):
- Y-axis: STRENGTH AND POTENCY OF NATURAL HUMAN DESIRE AS EVOLVED BEINGS
- X-axis: STRENGTH AND POTENCY OF RELIGIOUS SHAMING
- Labels along line (bottom to top): PRIDE, OCCASIONAL DESIRE FOR GLUTTONY, LUST OR BASIC SEXUAL DESIRE (THOUGHT CRIMES), SAME SEX ATTRACTION, SEX

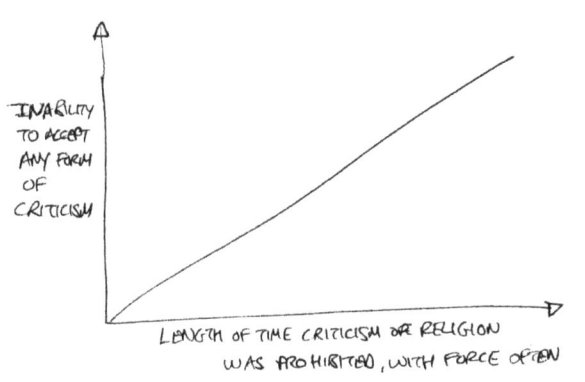

Chart 2 (axes):
- Y-axis: INABILITY TO ACCEPT ANY FORM OF CRITICISM
- X-axis: LENGTH OF TIME CRITICISM OF RELIGION WAS PROHIBITED, WITH FORCE OFTEN

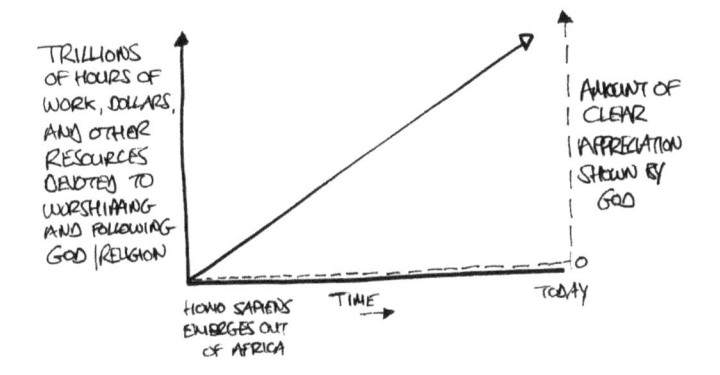

Chart 3 (axes):
- Left Y-axis: TRILLIONS OF HOURS OF WORK, DOLLARS, AND OTHER RESOURCES DEVOTED TO WORSHIPPING AND FOLLOWING GOD/RELIGION
- Right Y-axis: AMOUNT OF CLEAR APPRECIATION SHOWN BY GOD
- X-axis: TIME — from HOMO SAPIENS EMERGES OUT OF AFRICA to TODAY

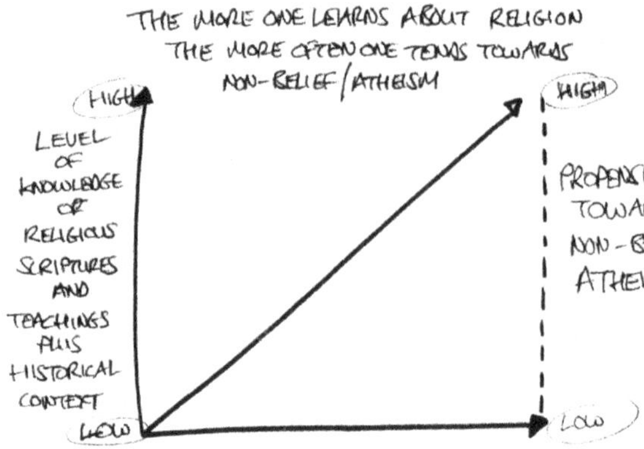
THE MORE ONE LEARNS ABOUT RELIGION
THE MORE OFTEN ONE TENDS TOWARDS
NON-BELIEF / ATHEISM
HIGH
LEVEL OF KNOWLEDGE OF RELIGIOUS SCRIPTURES AND TEACHINGS PLUS HISTORICAL CONTEXT
LOW
HIGH
PROPENSITY TOWARDS NON-BELIEF/ ATHEISM
LOW

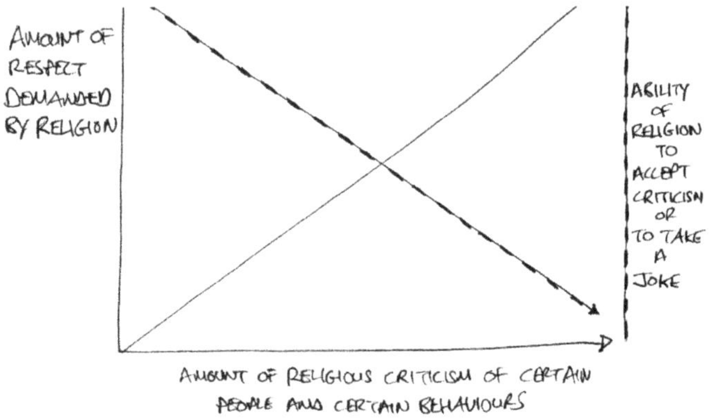
AMOUNT OF RESPECT DEMANDED BY RELIGION
ABILITY OF RELIGION TO ACCEPT CRITICISM OR TO TAKE A JOKE
AMOUNT OF RELIGIOUS CRITICISM OF CERTAIN PEOPLE AND CERTAIN BEHAVIOURS

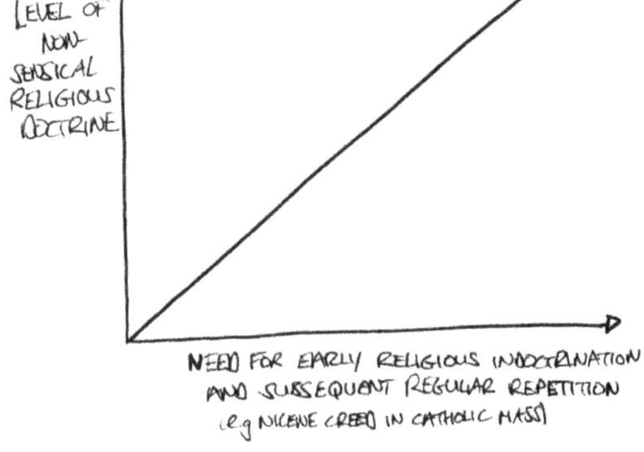
LEVEL OF NON-SENSICAL RELIGIOUS DOCTRINE
NEED FOR EARLY RELIGIOUS INDOCTRINATION AND SUBSEQUENT REGULAR REPETITION
(e.g NICENE CREED IN CATHOLIC MASS)

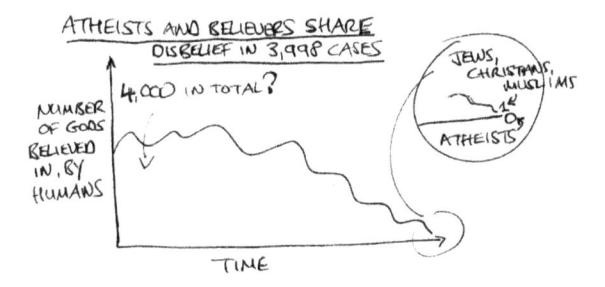

Atheists and believers are not too far apart. Both sets of people are atheists with regards to the approximately 4,000 other Gods who have been worshipped by humans in the past, in that they do not believe in them. Atheists just go one step/God further.

18. Religion gets in the way

Religion and religious apologists often use fear to control: fear of punishment in this life, of being ostracised, of being left out of an eternal reward, of damnation, among others. I would have been far too scared to even contemplate doing the following when I was a believer, but now I am more than happy to do so.

Thousands of deities from human history are no longer believed in, and have, to some extent, been discarded. Perhaps belief in the Gods of the Abrahamic religions will also go the same way?

RELIGION GETS IN THE WAY OF GLOBAL CHALLENGES

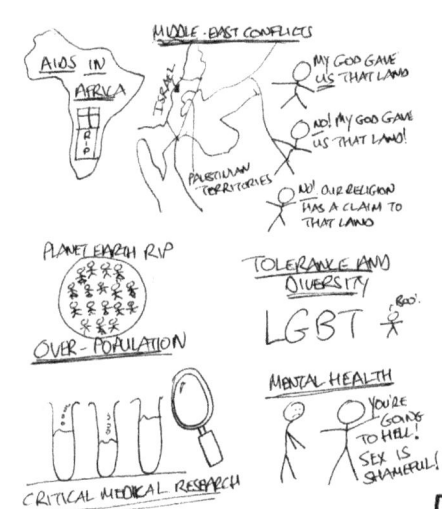

- AIDS IN AFRICA
- MIDDLE-EAST CONFLICTS
  - "MY GOD GAVE US THAT LAND!"
  - "NO! MY GOD GAVE US THAT LAND!"
  - "NO! OUR RELIGION HAS A CLAIM TO THAT LAND"
  - ISRAEL / PALESTINIAN TERRITORIES
- PLANET EARTH RIP
- OVER-POPULATION
- TOLERANCE AND DIVERSITY
  - LGBT — "Boo!"
- MENTAL HEALTH
  - "YOU'RE GOING TO HELL! SEX IS SHAMEFUL!"
- CRITICAL MEDICAL RESEARCH

MEMO TO GOD

TO: GOD
FROM: HUMANITY
SUBJECT: ADVICE PLEASE!
DATE: JANUARY 2018

RSVP

DEAR GOD,

LONG TIME NO SEE/HEAR!

THINGS ARE GETTING TRICKY DOWN HERE ON EARTH WITH LOTS OF PEOPLE KILLING EACH OTHER CLAIMING THEY KNOW WHAT YOU REALLY WANT FROM US.

PLEASE SEND US SOME CLARITY ON YOUR THINKING ABOUT WHAT YOU WANT FROM US BY END OF JULY 2018 AT THE LATEST. IF WE DON'T HEAR FROM YOU BY THEN WE WILL ASSUME YOU ARE NOT REALLY THAT INTERESTED IN US (NO OFFENCE WILL BE TAKEN, JUST GOOD TO KNOW!)

GRATEFUL FOR A CLEAR AND SPECIFIC RESPONSE FROM YOU (RATHER THAN USING A MAN IN A DESERT-BASED KINGDOM).

WITH LOVE AND RESPECT,
YOUR CHILDREN

WHAT HAS RELIGION TAUGHT US OR DONE FOR US COMPARED WITH RATIONAL, EVIDENCE-BASED SCIENCE?

*From the Atlantic Magazine

RELIGION	SCIENCE*
YOU'RE A SINNER	PRINTING PRESS
GAYS ARE BAD	ELECTRICITY
KILLING IS WRONG (PRETTY OBVIOUS)	PENICILLIN
	SEMI-CONDUCTOR ELECTRONICS
SEX IS SHAMEFUL	OPTICAL LENSES
LOVE YOUR ENEMY (IMPOSSIBLE)	VACCINATIONS
TURN THE OTHER CHEEK	THE INTERNET
	THE STEAM ENGINE
YOU CAN LIVE FOREVER	SANITATION
WOMEN CAN'T BE TRUSTED	REFRIGERATION
THE UNIVERSE WAS MADE IN 7 DAYS	THE AIRPLANE
	THE COMPASS
DEAD PEOPLE WILL RISE OUT OF THEIR GRAVES	CARS
	COMPUTERS
HUMAN SACRIFICE IS ACCEPTABLE	NUCLEAR FISSION
	TELEPHONE
BELIEF WITHOUT EVIDENCE IS ADMIRABLE	CEMENT AND STEEL MAKING
JESUS DIED FOR YOU, BUT HE IS STILL ALIVE	TELEVISION
	ANESTHESIA
GOD WILL COME SOON (2,000 YEARS LATE SO FAR)	MODERN MEDICINE
SNAKES CAN TALK	THE WHEEL
ETC.	ETC.

My view of religion now:

WE SHOULD BE ABLE TO TREAT RELIGION IN THE SAME WAY AS POLITICS, SPORT, PHILOSOPHY, CULTURAL MATTERS ETC

WITH SATIRE, HUMOUR, AND, WHEN NECESSARY, WITH RIDICULE AND CONTEMPT, AND I CLAIM THE RIGHT TO DO SO #CLAIMTHATRIGHT

THOSE PESKY HUMANS ARE MAKING FUN OF ME AGAIN AND IT'S NOT FAIR — I HAVE FEELINGS TOO YOU KNOW!

WOULD THE ALL POWERFUL CREATOR OF THE UNIVERSE REALLY BE UPSET WITH THIS? IF SO, IT'S HIS PROBLEM, AND THEN HE'S NOT WORTH WORSHIPPING ANYWAY.

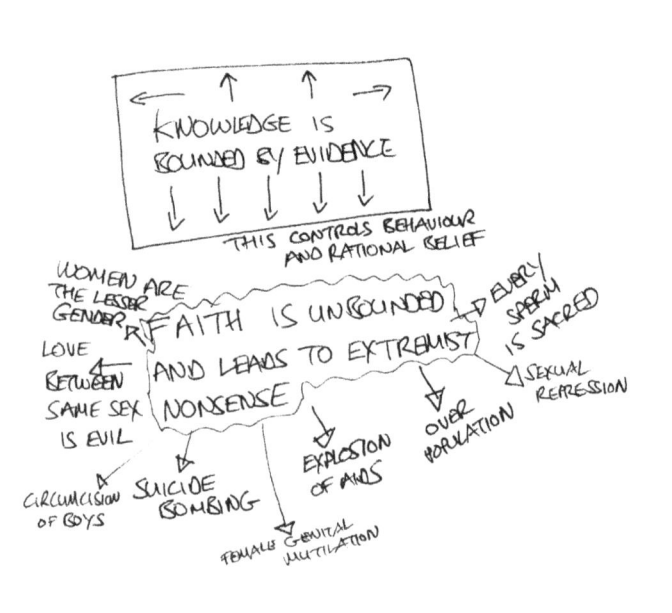

KNOWLEDGE IS BOUNDED BY EVIDENCE
THIS CONTROLS BEHAVIOUR AND RATIONAL BELIEF

WOMEN ARE THE LESSER GENDER

FAITH IS UNBOUNDED AND LEADS TO EXTREMIST NONSENSE

EVERY SPERM IS SACRED

LOVE BETWEEN SAME SEX IS EVIL

SEXUAL REPRESSION

CIRCUMCISION OF BOYS

SUICIDE BOMBING

EXPLOSION OF AIDS

OVER POPULATION

FEMALE GENITAL MUTILATION

CHURCH CELEBRATE THE BRUTAL MURDER OF A MAN WHO IS THREE PEOPLE AND ONE AT THE SAME TIME!

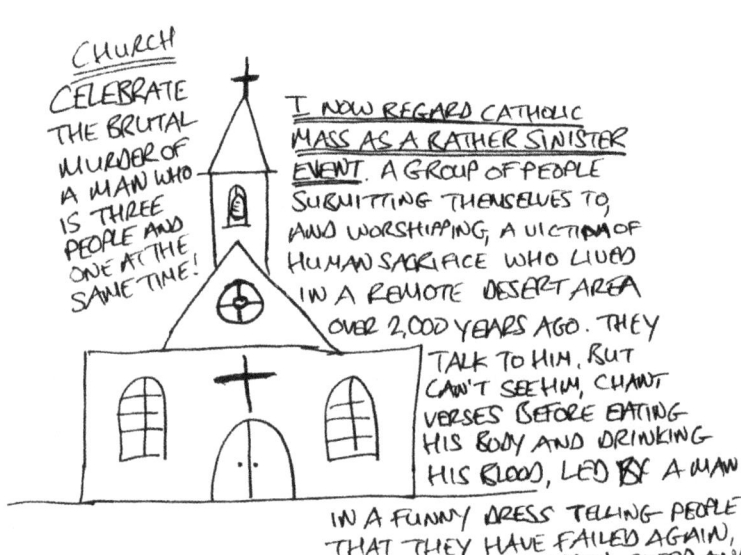

I NOW REGARD CATHOLIC MASS AS A RATHER SINISTER EVENT. A GROUP OF PEOPLE SUBMITTING THEMSELVES TO, AND WORSHIPPING, A VICTIM OF HUMAN SACRIFICE WHO LIVED IN A REMOTE DESERT AREA OVER 2,000 YEARS AGO. THEY TALK TO HIM, BUT CAN'T SEE HIM, CHANT VERSES BEFORE EATING HIS BODY AND DRINKING HIS BLOOD, LED BY A MAN IN A FUNNY DRESS TELLING PEOPLE THAT THEY HAVE FAILED AGAIN, CALLING THEM CHILDREN, SHEEP AND SLAVES

AND ALMOST NO-ONE QUESTIONS THIS AS BEING THE REMOTEST BIT WEIRD OR ANACHRONISTIC!?

19. Much better to be an amazing primate than a fallen angel

IT'S MUCH BETTER TO BE AN AMAZING PRIMATE, A CHILD OF THE UNIVERSE, 14 BILLION YEARS IN THE MAKING IN TOTAL

THE BIG BANG

ELEMENTS FORGED IN ENORMOUS SUPERNOVA EXPLOSIONS BECOMING A VITAL PART OF US

BOOM! → CARBON! → OXYGEN! → NITROGEN

I'M ALIVE!

PRODUCING US, CHILDREN OF STARS

FOLLOWED BY 4 BILLION YEARS OF GRADUAL EVOLUTION CULMINATING IN US, OUR UNIVERSE MADE CONSCIOUS

THE PINNACLE

AMAZING, INCREDIBLE, BEAUTIFUL PRIMATES

THAN TO JUST BE THE CHILD OF AN ANGRY, JEALOUS OLD DADDY WHO CURSED OUR ALLEGED ANCESTORS, AND US, FOR EATING THE FRUIT OF KNOWLEDGE

REDEEM YOURSELF CHILD!

God

ALL KNEEL BEFORE THE ALMIGHTY

I AM NOT WORTHY TO RECEIVE YOU

I MUST GO TO CONFESSION MORE

A FLAWED HUMAN

GOD FORGIVE US OUR TRESPASSES

JUST SAY THE WORD AND I SHALL BE HEALED

I AM JUST A POOR, WORTHLESS SINNER

4,000 YEARS IN THE MAKING, ALWAYS DOOMED TO DISAPPOINT HIS FATHER

Part 3

Finding my own way in life

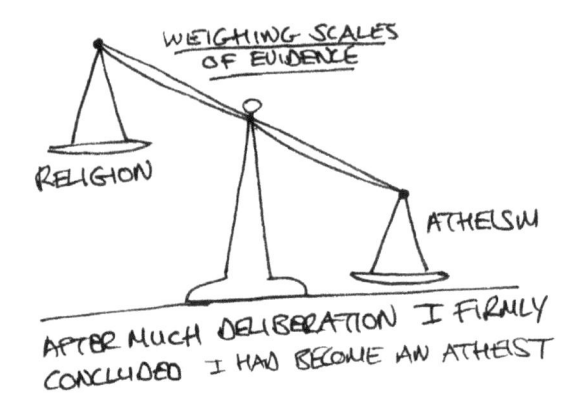

[Drawing: Weighing scales of evidence, with "RELIGION" side down and "ATHEISM" side up. Caption: "AFTER MUCH DELIBERATION I FIRMLY CONCLUDED I HAD BECOME AN ATHEIST"]

1. Leaving religion is liberating, but daunting

[Drawing of a stick figure with labels: "I'M FREE!", "BUT NOW I MUST FACE THE STARK REALITY OF EXISTENCE...", "THIS WAS A HUGELY LIBERATING BUT DAUNTING EXPERIENCE", "BY MYSELF, BUT I RESPECT AND LOVE MYSELF FOR HAVING THE COURAGE TO DO SO."]

I slowly felt very liberated, as if I was coming out from under a large, heavy cloud, into the sunshine. I realised I no longer had to adhere to a certain set of rules or a certain way of behaving, which I previously followed without question, and in which I had no input. My mind was suddenly able to think for itself, unencumbered by the need to appease, or please a separate entity. I also felt grown up suddenly, like leaving my parents' home for the first time, able to stand on my own two feet. This was both exciting and daunting. For all its faults, religion had given me a framework within which to exist mentally, a scaffold to hold my mind in place. Now this had all come down. Would I be able to live without it? I quickly realised though that I was free to define for myself my moral and ethical beliefs, and that I could continue to refine these as I read, reflected and learned more about life. I also realised fully that I have a very good sense of what is right and wrong within me, a great and reliable internal moral compass, which I had overlooked for so long in favour of religion. There is so much human knowledge out there, from so many sources, to help one find one's way in life. I read some basic philosophy and I found the concept of existentialism especially attractive. I also found much to enjoy and be inspired by in humanism. The views of the German philosopher Friedrich Nietzsche are particularly revelatory for me.

This sense of liberation gave me a huge sense of self-respect. I had freed myself from a delusion that I hadn't even realised I was in. It's only when I experienced the feeling of mental freedom that I realised what a mental and psychological straightjacket I had been living in. I had worked my way out of a huge mental maze, a maze where many hundreds of millions of other people remain trapped. I do not mean this in an arrogant way whatsoever. I was just lucky enough to be forced into questioning my beliefs in a stringent manner.

I also now realise that deep down I think I had always doubted religion to some extent, but I was too deeply immersed in it at too young an age to ever recognise this. This led to a subconscious self-deception. To me, self-deception is a crime inflicted on the self. Lying to oneself (something that all humans are capable of to quite an extraordinary degree) eats away at your self-respect, your trust in yourself, your moral bearings, your ability to understand yourself, your ability to emotionally understand others, your self-acceptance and your basic sense of dignity. These attributes all return when the self-deception comes to an end.In addition, I started seeing the world from a different, clearer perspective. I had a renewed sense of vitality and wonder for life, the only one I will ever have. I felt I had much more control over my life; that I was no longer dependent on someone else.

2. Replacing the false friend of religion – some words on atheism, existentialism and humanism

[Figure: Four stick figures showing progression:
- "I MUST BE DUTIFUL TO GOD TO ENTER HEAVEN. I WAS BORN SINFUL" — CONFUSED, SINFUL BELIEVER
- "I'M FREE!" — LIBERATED ATHEIST
- "I'M RESPONSIBLE FOR ESTABLISHING MEANING IN MY LIFE AND FOR ALL MY ACTIONS" (EXISTENCE PRECEDES ESSENCE) — RESPONSIBLE EXISTENTIALIST
- "I ENJOY A WORLD VIEW BASED ON CARE, COMPASSION, AND A SENSE OF WONDER. ONE LIFE, LIVE IT WELL!" — GROUNDED HUMANIST]

Friedrich Nietzsche

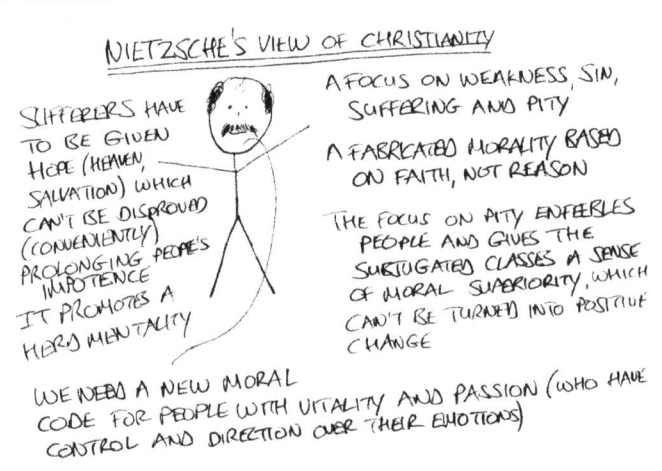

[Figure: NIETZSCHE'S VIEW OF CHRISTIANITY
- SUFFERERS HAVE TO BE GIVEN HOPE (HEAVEN, SALVATION) WHICH CAN'T BE DISPROVED (CONVENIENTLY), PROLONGING PEOPLE'S IMPOTENCE
- IT PROMOTES A HERD MENTALITY
- A FOCUS ON WEAKNESS, SIN, SUFFERING AND PITY
- A FABRICATED MORALITY BASED ON FAITH, NOT REASON
- THE FOCUS ON PITY ENFEEBLES PEOPLE AND GIVES THE SUBJUGATED CLASSES A SENSE OF MORAL SUPERIORITY, WHICH CAN'T BE TURNED INTO POSITIVE CHANGE
- WE NEED A NEW MORAL CODE FOR PEOPLE WITH VITALITY AND PASSION (WHO HAVE CONTROL AND DIRECTION OVER THEIR EMOTIONS)]

(From an article by William Al-Sharif, published in 2006 https://archive.org/stream/ NietzcheAndChristianValues/Nietzsche_djvu.txt)

EXISTENTIALISM (FOR ME)

I'M FREE! (ALTHOUGH I AM FULLY RESPONSIBLE FOR ALL MY ACTIONS)

WITH DISCIPLINE AND RESPONSIBILITY I FIND OUT AND DEFINE WHO I AM

I'M FINDING MY AUTHENTIC SELF

RELIGIOUS RULES ARE ARBITRARY SO NO MORE ORIGINAL SIN

Atheism is the absence of belief in deities. Why aren't there also words for an absence of belief in other things?

ALOCHNESSMONSTERISM

ATHEISM
GOD?

ASUPERSTITIOUSISM

AFATHERCHRISTMASISM

A FAIRY ISM

AGHOSTISM

AFLYINGSAUCERISM

AYETIISM

3. Some concluding remarks

To summarise briefly, I was a believer in the doctrines of the Roman Catholic faith, or Catholic Christianity. I am now an atheist in the sense that I do not believe in the existence of a supernatural being stemming from the Abrahamic religions, the biggest of which are Judaism, Christianity and Islam (I just do not find their teachings plausible). I would place myself at present on rung 6 of Richard Dawkins' spectrum of theistic probability, namely a "de facto atheist. Very low probability, but short of zero. 'I don't know for certain, but I think God is very improbable, and I live my life on the assumption that he is not there'". (https://en.wikipedia.org/wiki/Spectrum_of_theistic_probability#Dawkins'_formulation.)

Like many atheists in this sense, I remain open to the idea of a supernatural deity who is interested in human affairs should sufficient evidence become available.

Part 4

Selected reading

Sarah Bakewell, *At The Existentialist Café: Freedom, Being, and Apricot Cocktails*, Other Press 2016

Gary Bakker, *God: A Psychological Assessment*, Universal 2013

Dan Barker, *God: The Most Unpleasant Character in All Fiction*, Sterling 2016

Sean Carroll, *The Big Picture: On the Origins of Life, Meaning, and the Universe Itself*, Dutton 2017

Peter Catapano, Simon Critchley, *The Stone Reader: Modern Philosophy in 133 Arguments*, Liveright 2015

Richard Dawkins, *The God Delusion*, Black Swan 2006

Bart D. Ehrman, *God's Problem: How the Bible Fails to Answer Our Most Important Question – Why We Suffer*, HarperCollins 2008; *Jesus Interrupted: Revealing the Hidden Contradictions in the Bible*, HarperCollins 2009

Sam Harris, *Letter To A Christian Nation*, Vintage 2006

Christopher Hitchens, *God is Not Great: How Religion Poisons Everything*, Hachette 2007; *The Portable Atheist: Essential Readings for the Non-Believer*, Da Capo 2007

Richard Holloway, *A Little History of Religion*, Yale University Press 2016

Dorling Kindersley, *The Religions Book (Big Ideas Simply Explained)*, DK 2013; with Will Buckingham, *The Philosophy Book*, DK 2011

Joan Konner, *The Atheist's Bible: An Illustrious Collection of Irreverent Thoughts*, HarperCollins 2007

Lawrence M Krauss, *A Universe from Nothing*, Free Press 2012

E.A. Livingstone, ed. *Concise Oxford Dictionary of the Christian Church*, Oxford University Press, 2006

Christopher Panza, *Existentialism For Dummies*, Wiley 2008

Michael Rosen, *What is Humanism? How Do You Live Without a God? And Other Big Questions for Kids*, Wayland 2015

Peter Singer, *Ethics in the Real World: 82 Brief Essays on Things That Matter*, Princeton 2016

Nigel Warburton, *A Little History of Philosophy*, Yale University Press 2011

If you liked this book I would really appreciate you adding a quick review of it on your favourite sites (it shouldn't take more than a few minutes) and thanks in advance for considering this!

For more information on Luke and his work please go to www.lukepemberton.com

Lightning Source UK Ltd.
Milton Keynes UK
UKHW01f1427050718
325283UK00001B/116/P